FREEDOM AT RISK

The Kidnapping
of Free Blacks
in America,
1780-1865

CAROL WILSON

THE UNIVERSITY PRESS OF KENTUCKY

Copyright © 1994 by The University Press of Kentucky

Scholarly publisher for the Commonwealth,
serving Bellarmine College, Berea College, Centre
College of Kentucky, Eastern Kentucky University,
The Filson Club, Georgetown College, Kentucky
Historical Society, Kentucky State University,
Morehead State University, Murray State University,
Northern Kentucky University, Transylvania University,
University of Kentucky, University of Louisville,
and Western Kentucky University.

Editorial and Sales Offices: Lexington, Kentucky 40508-4008

Library of Congress Cataloging-in-Publication Data

Wilson, Carol, 1962-
    Freedom at Risk : the kidnapping of free Blacks in America,
1780-1865 / Carol Wilson.
        p.   cm.
    Includes bibliographical references (p.   ) and index.
    ISBN 0-8131-1858-1 (alk. paper)
    1. Afro-Americans—History—To 1863. 2. Kidnapping—United
States—History—18th century. 3. Kidnapping—United States—
History—19th century. 4. Afro-Americans—Legal status, laws, etc.
5. Slavery—United States. I. Title.
E185.18.W55   1994
973'.0496073—dc20   93-21012

Contents

Acknowledgments

The completion of this work was facilitated by many people. John R. McKivigan gave careful attention to the manuscript and contributed many useful suggestions. Rosemarie Zagarri offered valuable advice throughout the process. Thanks are due as well to the Interlibrary Loan Staff of West Virginia University, especially Judi McCracken, for consistently and cheerfully providing me with sources not easily accessible.

I would also like to thank Robert Fallaw and my colleagues in the Department of History at Washington College for their support and encouragement. Emilie Amt merits special mention for her greatly valued assistance with computer matters. I am grateful to all at the University Press of Kentucky for their prompt and fair handling of the manuscript.

My parents, Calvin D. and Lois W. Wilson, have continually supported my work, and my father's enthusiasm for and interest in the project has been especially appreciated. Robert L. Zangrando first suggested the topic of kidnapping to me. His comments on several parts of the book were invaluable, and his encouragement throughout my career has been stimulating and inspiring.

Most of all, the quality of this project is the result of the patient editing and professional guidance of Ronald L. Lewis. Many years ago, he nurtured a young student in whom few others saw potential; for that I will be forever indebted to him.

Introduction

The kidnapping of free blacks into slavery in pre-Civil War America has been a topic frequently noted by scholars but not examined in any detail. This omission may be partly explained by the fact that while slavery has long been a subject of intense interest for both scholars and the general public, comparatively less work has focused on free blacks. However, a significant body of scholarship now provides an image of the diversity of black life before the Civil War. Whether northern or southern, rural or urban, escaped or manumitted slaves, or the descendants of generations of free-born people, black Americans all shared one disadvantage: they did not enjoy the same rights, privileges, and opportunities as white Americans. Constrained by a lack of economic and educational opportunity, the absence of legal protection, overbearing legal restrictions, and the contempt of whites, free blacks were in fact "slaves without masters," as Ira Berlin has characterized them.[1]

This study examines another aspect of discrimination against free blacks. The kidnapping of free blacks for sale as slaves was an all-too-common occurrence in the United States during the decades between the Revolution and the Civil War. The ever-present danger of kidnapping and the fact that its victims had little recourse proved a grave threat to the black community.

What made the practice of kidnapping possible was the strong and deeply rooted belief in white superiority. One of the great debates in African-American history has centered on the question of which came first, racism or slavery. Scholars such as T.H. Breen and Stephen Innes have argued that blacks in seventeenth century Virginia did not face unilateral discrimination; rather, racism came only with the increased demand for labor and rise in the black population. The legal code that identified blacks as slaves in the American colonies was not put into place until the 1670s, and its rationale was economic, not philosophic.[2] Although legal manifestation of racist beliefs was delayed, Winthrop Jordan has traced the development of racial prejudice among the English to the sixteenth century. Even before contact with black people, English men and women had formed a concept of black as something negative, frightening, even evil. When they encountered Africans, this belief was then applied to them. Difference in appearance, when magnified by other differences, particularly religious, led the British to loathe and fear Africans.[3]

Racial prejudice accompanied the English and other European colonists, along with their African slaves, to the New World. As the numbers of blacks increased, so did racist proscriptions against them. As the colonists created new lives for themselves and eventually established a new nation, they fashioned a legal system to support their belief in white superiority and to protect slavery, including the recovery of fugitives. Coupled with the lack of effective legal safeguards and due process for black Americans, either slave or free, the system actually facilitated kidnapping, even though the practice was illegal in most states.

The greed of kidnappers was one cause of the crime. The demand for labor assured a high market price for slaves, especially after the invention of the cotton gin, the abolition of the African slave trade, and the opening of new land in the Southwest. The apathy and ignorance of the majority of the white population, who did nothing to prevent the practice, also greatly encouraged kidnapping. But not all whites ignored the crime. Some government officials and private citizens, northern and southern, worked to prevent kidnapping and to free those illegally enslaved. By far, abolitionists offered the greatest hope for victims of kidnapping. However, blacks all too often found these avenues of assistance blocked, and they thus organized for protection within their own communities.

Some explanation of the use of the term *kidnapping* is necessary. Today we generally assume the word to refer to the seizure of a person, by force or through enticement, followed by a demand for ransom to ensure his or her return. In this study, the term kidnapping applies to a similar practice within the specific historical situation in which free black persons were seized for sale into slavery. Instead of receiving ransom from the victim's family or friends, or demanding a political exchange of prisoners held by a target nation, or "reclaiming" offspring held by a former spouse, kidnappers in this instance benefited financially from the sale of a free black person into slavery.

Kidnapping as used here must also be distinguished from several other historical uses of the term. The kidnapping of free black Americans must be viewed as part of a larger picture of kidnapping over time and space. Although it is beyond the scope of this study, certainly the kidnapping of African peoples to supply the slave trade represents one of the largest and most devastating forms of kidnapping in history. Many of the 10 million victims of the African slave trade were taken from their homes, usually along the West Coast of Africa, and sold as slaves to Europeans throughout the Americas.[4]

Other forms of kidnapping threatened whites also. Probably most common was the impressment of Americans during the colonial and early national eras for service in the British navy. While one may dismiss the experience of young David Balfour in Robert Louis Stevenson's famous novel *Kidnapped* as simply entertaining fiction, in fact the practice of kidnapping men for service on naval vessels "had been strongly relied on as a means of manning the British navy in all the wars in which that nation was engaged during the seventeenth and eighteenth centuries." One of the causes of the War of 1812, impressment was ended thereafter.[5]

Whites were kidnapped also to help populate English colonies. Edmund Morgan has estimated that many of the sailors and settlers of the Roanoke colony were impressed or "spirited" from their homes in England. "Spirits" lured adults with liquor, children with candy, and earned a pound or two from ship captains for each unwilling passenger. The captains themselves were often more directly involved, abducting "desperate men, whether in jail or out, . . . and men too drunk to know what they were doing." Once in the colonies, unemployed men also found themselves impressed into military service. Although the prevalence of the practice of kidnapping has been debated, many of this country's first settlers did not come willingly, and there is evidence that kidnapping became an established enterprise in parts of England.[6] According to Eric Williams, "As commercial speculation entered the picture, abuses crept in. Kidnapping was encouraged to a great degree and became a regular business in such towns as London and Bristol."[7]

Perhaps most appalling by modern standards was the kidnapping of English children for labor in the colonies. In the early seventeenth century, the City of London reached an agreement with the Virginia Company of London to remove a "large number of vagrant children" who "formed a rowdy element there responsible for much of the disorder and petty crime that plagued the city." Because of this negative characterization of the orphans, the practice was accepted as a means of dealing with the orphan population.[8]

Kidnapping had precedents in the forcing of European whites into naval and colonial servitude, and in the abduction of African peoples into American slavery. Thus the kidnapping of free blacks into slavery in the United States during the eighteenth and nineteenth centuries was not an historical anomaly. Although the type of kidnapping examined in this book exhibited its own particular characteristics, it, like the conditions it embraced, slavery and freedom, was not an aberration.

In the American pre–Civil War usage, the term kidnapping applied to various types of abduction. For the most part, this book explores actual and attempted incidents of kidnapping of free blacks into slavery in the United States. Contemporary accounts most commonly used the term in this manner, but antislavery advocates occasionally used the term kidnapping, particularly after 1850, to describe the efforts of slaveholders to return fugitives to bondage. Abolitionist Henry C. Wright, for example, used the term in this manner when he declared, "Death to Kidnappers!"[9]

Militant critics of slavery also used *kidnapped* to mark the status of all black Americans held to forced labor. Noting that slaves had originally been taken against their will from Africa, these abolitionists argued that they and their descendants all were victims of kidnapping and were, therefore, illegally held in bondage. "The Firebrand—By An Incendiary Fanatic," a column written for William Lloyd Garrison's *Liberator*, asserted, "We hold it to be a self-evident truth, that every slave in the United States has been kidnapped."[10] In an earlier column, "The Firebrand" had claimed, "The holder of that slave is a Man-stealer, or an accessory, or a receiver of stolen goods, or a purchaser of a human being whom he knew was stolen."[11]

The term also was used by pro-slavery advocates to refer to the practice of helping slaves escape to the North. The *New Orleans Mercantile Advertiser* complained: "It was thought kidnapping was not practised here. To the sorrow of many of our own citizens the contrary is the fact, and not a season of sickness passes, but that twenty or thirty slaves are carried off by vessels to the North. We do not charge this upon the masters of boats or vessels. For we cannot believe they would act in this manner, but our opinion leads us to suppose that even they are made the dupes of a set of canting scoundrels, who under the cloak of humanity rob their fellow creatures of their all."[12]

Slaves were also stolen in the South for sale in other parts of that region. Slave stealing was not legally kidnapping because the slave was deemed by law to be property rather than a person. It was much easier to kidnap a free black to sell into slavery than to seize a slave, whose master was likely to come looking for his stolen property.[13] Therefore, slave stealing probably occurred infrequently.

This book will focus only on the efforts to force into slavery black people who were legally free, either by enslaving the freeborn or by reenslaving those who had been manumitted or who had purchased their freedom. It will not examine the more widely known subject of fugitive slaves who escaped from bondage only to be captured and returned to their masters, as required by law. [14]

It is impossible to know the number of free blacks who were kidnapped into slavery, much less those who were victims of attempted kidnappings. Because kidnapping was a crime, efforts were made by all but the most brazen kidnappers to conceal their actions. As U.B. Phillips noted in his classic treatise, *American Negro Slavery*, "Kidnappings without pretense of legal claim were done so furtively that they seldom attained record unless the victims had recourse to the courts; and this was made rare by the helplessness of childhood in some cases and in others by the fear of lashes." [15] Once kidnappers sold their captives into slavery, the chances of the victim's free status being revealed were reduced even further. An enslaved free black was dependent upon a sympathetic white ear to make any headway in the battle toward restoring freedom. Certainly slaveowners would be reluctant to believe that a newly purchased slave was legally free. It can be assumed that only the most scrupulous would investigate allegations of kidnapping carefully, especially when the result might well be financial loss and even possible criminal prosecution.

Kidnappers physically abused and pyschologically terrorized their captives into stating that they were slaves. If they were beaten again by their new masters for claiming free status, it is easy to see that many stories of kidnapping would never be told. Therefore, few, if any, records exist of the many kidnapped free blacks who probably lived out their lives in illegal bondage. Even if a kidnapped slave succeeded in convincing a white person of his or her story, few white southerners would be willing to expend time and money, as well as incurring the wrath of their neighbors, in pressing the victim's case. Solomon Northup, perhaps the best-known kidnapping victim, who published his life story upon his return to freedom after more than a decade in slavery, noted, "I doubt not hundreds have been as unfortunate as myself; that hundreds of free citizens have been kidnapped and sold into slavery, and are at this moment wearing out their lives on plantations in Texas and Louisiana."[16]

Nor did success in gaining the attention of authorities guarantee the restoration of freedom. Even when an incident of kidnapping was recognized and resulted in a trial, the great difficulty of verifying a black's freedom to the satisfaction of whites remained. In the eyes of most whites, all blacks were presumed to be slaves unless they could demonstrate otherwise, and providing legal proof was often impossible. Not all blacks carried freedom papers, and those who were kidnapped had often been robbed of their papers. Even in some court cases, judges dismissed free papers as evidence, claiming that they could be easily forged. Witnesses also presented a problem. In most cases, blacks could not testify against whites. Therefore, victims and their families and friends were excluded from the legal process. Only a white witness could attest to a black's freedom, and those who might have been willing to help were frequently prevented from testifying for a black against a white because they feared retribution by other whites. Even if such a person testified, restoration of freedom was not guaranteed. Whether or not a legitimate case was presented, judges and juries hesitated to convict the kidnapper.

Racism is another factor that hinders an accurate assessment of the extent of kidnapping. Since kidnapping was a crime usually committed by whites against blacks, a large segment of the white population did not find it particularly troubling. Abolitionist John Parrish noted in 1806, "We permit six hundred persons to be kidnapped in six months alone because people want to get rid of the free Negroes."[17] And because whites were almost exclusively the record-keepers of American society before the Civil War, many areas of black life have either been left out of the historical record or have been included in a distorted fashion. But, although it may be

sparse, there is a record from both blacks and whites, kidnappers and victims, southerners and northerners, abolitionists
and politicians, sufficient to indicate the nature, extent, and
significance of kidnapping. We know that it occurred over a
geographical area covering virtually the entire settled United
States, from the earliest years of the Republic through the
Civil War.[18] Numerous observers of American life noted the
grave threat that kidnapping posed. Philadelphia abolitionist
Thomas P. Cope, for example, related in his diary in 1803,
"Not a day passes but free blacks are stolen by force or decoyed by the most wicked artifices from the Northern and
Middle States and sold for slaves in the Southern."[19]

Indeed, kidnapping was a problem substantial enough to
warrant government attention on the local, state, and federal
levels. The issue was debated more than once in Congress
and even more frequently in statehouses. Abolition societies
throughout the country offered assistance to victims of kidnapping and fought vigorously to prevent the crime from
continuing. The black community worked through legal
channels by lobbying officials for better protection and by
initiating lawsuits to restore victims' freedom and prosecute
kidnappers. When those tactics met with unsatisfactory results, blacks armed for self-defense.

Chapter 1 of this book examines the phenomenon of direct
abduction and explains the circumstances surrounding this
type of free black enslavement. It also provides a view of
who the kidnappers were and how they operated, focusing
particularly on what was probably the largest kidnapping
ring in the country. Chapter 2 looks at forms of "legal" kidnapping and demonstrates how some free blacks were enslaved not through forceful abduction but through federal
and state laws such as the fugitive slave laws and the Negro
seamen acts. Chapter 3 focuses on efforts through the legal
system to protect blacks from kidnapping, particularly the
efforts of several public officials. Abolitionist participation in
the antikidnapping crusade is detailed in chapter 4, and chapter 5 examines the response within the black community to
kidnapping.

"From Their Free Homes into Bondage": The Abduction of Free Blacks into Slavery

The possibility of being kidnapped and sold into slavery was shared by the entire American free black community, whether young or old, freeborn or freed slave, northerner or southerner. Certainly, however, some were at greater risk than others. Geography may have been the most important factor influencing the degree of risk. Although the practice occurred throughout the nation, residents of the states bordering the Mason-Dixon line were especially vulnerable. The large numbers of free blacks in Delaware, Maryland, and southern Pennsylvania, as well as proximity to the South, probably attracted kidnappers to this area.

Several factors other than geography determined the frequency of kidnapping. Age was another element. Children, presumably because they were easier to abduct than adults, were a favored target of kidnappers. Poverty was a third factor. Impoverished adults, desperate for income, were vulnerable to a kidnapper's deceptive offer of work. But again, no one was safe from the crime. Even several free blacks among the elite—financially secure and respected in their communities—encountered the specter of kidnapping.

The crime was pervasive partly because of the potential for great profits from a successful kidnapping and sale of a free black into slavery, which made many kidnappers willing to take the risks. In any case, kidnappers may have perceived no great risk, as the racism of the majority of American whites rendered it unlikely that kidnappers would be prosecuted to the full extent of the law. Although kidnapping was a crime in most states, it was a crime committed against blacks and therefore ignored by many whites.

Thus, kidnapping occurred throughout the country. One of the northernmost recorded kidnappings occurred in Sanbornton, New Hampshire, in 1836. The victim was a ten-year-old boy who had been placed with Noah Rollins by the overseers of the poor. For fifty dollars Rollins sold the child to an Alabama man named Bennett. Although the purchaser escaped, Rollins was jailed for kidnapping, and the boy was rescued.[1]

Possibly the southernmost known kidnapping occurred in Baton Rouge in 1860. Marguerite S. Fayman, a Creole girl from "people of wealth and prestige," was kidnapped at age ten. She had been living on a farm where her family raised pelicans, and she had attended a private school run by French nuns. The Sisters often took their young charges for walks around the port of Baton Rouge. Walking along the wharf on the Mississippi River one day, Marguerite became separated from the other children. A man grabbed her, took her aboard a nearby ship, and kept her in a cabin until the vessel sailed for Louisville. She remained a slave in Kentucky until her escape in 1864.[2]

The vast majority of kidnappings, however, took place not along the nation's perimeters but in the border states of Pennsylvania, Delaware, and Maryland. As Underground Railroad conductor Levi Coffin remembered, "Free negroes in Pennsylvania were frequently kidnapped or decoyed into these states [Virginia and Maryland], then hurried away to Georgia, Alabama, Louisiana and sold."[3] Lawyer and anti-slavery pamphleteer Jesse Torrey declared in 1818 that it would take a book to record all the incidences of kidnapping that had occurred in Delaware. Two years earlier, Torrey had testified before a U.S. House of Representatives committee about the numerous kidnappings in Delaware and Maryland of which he had personal knowledge.[4]

There are several reasons for the primacy of this area. Pennsylvania, Delaware, and Maryland combined had a greater free black population than the rest of the country combined from 1790 to 1860. Especially in the early nineteenth century, when many tobacco farmers in the Upper South began diversifying their crops and manumitting or selling their slaves, the free black populations of these states increased. Cities, particularly Philadelphia, saw a large percentage of this increase.[5]

Proximity to the Mason–Dixon line made it easy to transport victims into the South. Some kidnappers carried their victims southward by land, but many also took advantage of the Delaware River and the network of rivers leading into the Chesapeake Bay.[6] Moreover, the anonymity of the port cities of Philadelphia, Wilmington, and Baltimore facilitated kidnapping.

Kidnappers used a variety of methods. The most obvious means of enslaving a free person was direct, forceful abduction. Kidnappers simply took their victims by incapacitating them or by threatening violence. As earlier indicated, children were especially vulnerable in this regard. Henry Edwards, for example, as a young boy was spirited away by two kidnappers from Newtown, New Jersey, hidden in a wagon. In Bordentown, several miles away, the victim managed to gain the attention of passersby by kicking the wagon's side. They rescued him and the kidnappers fled.[7] Two free black men from Illinois were not so fortunate. Forced across the Mississippi River from Cairo by a Missouri gang, one escaped by swimming back across the river. He managed to find his way home, bleeding and "mangled about the head." As in numerous other cases, what happened to the second victim is unknown.[8]

Deceit was a ubiquitous element in adult kidnappings. Adults were frequently lured into a kidnapper's company by some pretext, then forcibly restrained and taken into slavery. Some kidnapping victims were attracted by the promise of a job. The case of Solomon Northup, probably the most famous kidnapping case, involved such deception. Northup was a free black man well known in New York state for his skill as a musician. Invited by two white entertainers to join their act, he traveled about the East Coast. Reaching the nation's capital, he was drugged by his companions and awak-

ened in a slave jail. sold to a dealer, Northup was sent to
Louisiana, where he labored as a slave for more than a decade
before he could get word to his wife, Anne. She secured the
aid of Washington Hunt, the governor of New York, in freeing her husband. En route to his home, Northup and his
lawyer stopped in Washington, D.C., and initiated prosecution of the slave trader who had sold Northup to New Orleans. James Burch was acquitted.[9] But the Cleveland *Leader*
reported in 1854 that it was thought that Northup's kidnapper (presumably one of the men who had lured him to Washington) had been captured. "If so, let the law deal with the
scoundrel in its utmost severity!"[10]

The offer of a job was not the only means kidnappers used
to lure victims, as antislavery writer Jesse Torrey heard from
one of several blacks he discovered chained in an attic in Washington, D.C. (As a slave-trading center, the nation's capital
was an especially threatening spot for people of color.) One of
the people he encountered there was a twenty-one-year-old
indentured servant, who had been decoyed from his home in
Delaware by the prospect of hunting possum with his master.
Once he was in the fields, two strangers seized, bound, and
threatened him with pistols. Eventually he was taken to Washington and sold, being beaten several times for insisting he was
not a slave.[11]

Blacks as well as whites were guilty of kidnapping. Two
especially tragic accounts of kidnappings performed by blacks
involved men who lured women with romantic advances.
Jesse Torrey described "a monster in human shape," a Philadelphia man who apparently married black women for the
purpose of selling them into slavery. When the city's black
population discovered his treachery, a mob attacked him, but
the police saved him from certain death by incarcerating him.[12]

A similar story was that of a woman known only as Lucinda, a young domestic in a small Illinois town about fifty miles
from the Missouri border. Formerly a slave in Kentucky, she
had "legally secured her freedom." Lucinda had been seeing a
barber in the town, although she had been warned about him.
He was described as "a decidedly dandyish fellow" who was

believed to be part black, although he claimed to be part Indian. Early one summer, a man who said he was from Maryland arrived in the Illinois town looking for a summer home. "And to those of us who were boys he 'looked exactly like a southerner,'" recalled resident George Murray McConnel, "but the real southerners by birth who lived in the village smiled, and said he was rather too tropical in style."[13]

The stranger made Lucinda's acquaintance and claimed he was a friend of her former master in Kentucky. She was also warned about him, but paid no heed. One day the barber took Lucinda for a drive. When they had not returned by sunset as expected, no one worried, thinking that the barber was proposing marriage. That night, however, an alarm was raised after the barber returned to town alone on horseback. One man said that the wagon in which the two had gone for a ride belonged to the southerner. Three men, including McConnel's father, confronted the barber, who first claimed that he had returned with Lucinda but changed his story when they threatened him. The barber said that several miles out of town he had gone into the woods for some sassafras root and when he returned, Lucinda and the wagon were gone. He had not notified the police because he thought she had abandoned him, and he was angry with her.[14]

Eventually the men caught up with Lucinda and the Marylander several miles outside of town. Others, having heard the story, joined them, and they all returned home, "a little triumphal procession." Lucinda backed up the barber's story, saying that she had been kidnapped after her escort went into the woods. No one believed the barber's innocence, and he left town shortly thereafter.[15]

As mentioned earlier, children were particularly vulnerable to kidnapping. Many were enslaved after being hired out by their parents, a common and economically necessary practice in the poor black community. Ira Berlin has argued that many blacks, especially children, were virtually enslaved under apprenticeship agreements. Even worse, these arrangements left children open to actual enslavement when they were sold by an unscrupulous employer.[16] Young Sarah Taylor (or Harrison) was begging in the streets of New York City when she came to the attention of Haley and Anna Howard in 1858. They persuaded her parents to let Sarah go with them to live in Newark, New Jersey, as their servant. Instead, they took the girl to Washington, D.C., where they attempted to sell her for six hundred dollars. When she related her story to the owner of the hotel where they were staying, Sarah won his protection. Sarah's case was brought to the attention of the mayor of New York City, who had her restored to her family. The Howards (their names turned out to be aliases) fled to Baltimore, but authorities caught up with and arrested them, and Haley Howard eventually served several months in prison for kidnapping.[17]

Another case involved six-year-old Peter Still and his eight-year-old brother, Levin, who were kidnapped in the early nineteenth century. Playing at their home near Philadelphia, the boys became concerned as the day wore on and their mother did not return home as expected. Deciding to go to the church to look for her, they accepted a ride with a stranger in a gig. He took them not to their mother but to Versailles, Kentucky. In nearby Lexington, they were taken to their new master's cook and told, "There is your mother." The boys were struck when they protested, and they quickly learned not to contradict their owner. They thought about their former home and freedom frequently, however, and although afraid to run away, they hoped to buy their freedom someday. Levin died a slave, but Peter Still eventually purchased his freedom and returned home after about forty years.[18]

Children were targets of kidnappers because they were easier to abduct forcibly than adults. William Wells Brown, abolitionist and author, wrote to *National Anti-Slavery Standard* editor Sydney Gay, apprising him of a kidnapping in Georgetown, Ohio, in 1844. Traveling through the town on his way to Mount Pleasant, Brown encountered "the citizens standing upon the corners of the streets talking as though something had occurred during the night." They told him that the night before, five or six men had broken into the home of John Wilkinson, beating him and his wife before carrying away their fourteen-year-old son. With the help of neighbors, Wilkinson pursued the kidnappers, who crossed the Ohio River into Virginia. It is not known whether the boy was recovered.[19]

If kidnapped at a very early age, a free black child might grow up a slave never knowing that he or she had been born free. Such was the case with Lavinia Bell. She was kidnapped as an infant in Washington, D.C., along with numerous others, by Tom Watson, who was eventually sentenced to life imprisonment in the Richmond Penitentiary. Bell learned of her free status from her mistress in Galveston, Texas, where she was brutally abused. After numerous attempts, Bell eventually escaped to Montreal, where her story was recorded.[20]

Another vulnerable group was blacks held as contraband during the Civil War. Legally slaves, they had been freed in effect by advancing Union troops, yet they existed in a legal limbo between free and slave status, a very precarious position. As nonslaves, they had no masters to protect them, but not being free they did not enjoy protection of the law. They were at the mercy of the Union soldiers, some of whom found selling them an easy way to make money.

Blacks held as contraband faced danger from soldiers of both sides during the Civil War. The abduction of sixteen-year-old Charles Amos and his younger cousin was not unusual. The two had hired out as servants to officers of the Forty-second Massachusetts Infantry Regiment, traveling with them to Galveston, Texas, late in 1862. After Confederate forces recaptured the town on the first day of the new year, the invaders sold Amos and his cousin into slavery.[21]

Cavalry units of the Army of Northern Virginia also kidnapped blacks, both slave and free, during the Pennsylvania campaign in June of 1863. By some accounts, this practice affected large numbers of black residents of southern part of the state. Edwin Coddington, author of a study of the Gettysburg campaign, claimed that "thousands" of free blacks fled the Cumberland Valley into Harrisburg seeking refuge from the troops. At least fifty Pennsylvania blacks were sent into slavery as a result of the campaign.[22]

While the kidnapping of blacks by Confederate soldiers is not surprising, their northern counterparts were guilty of the same crime. The activities of the Ninety-ninth Regiment, New York Volunteers, stationed near Deep Creek, Virginia, provide one illustration. Residents there had been suspicious for some time that the soldiers had been "capturing stray contrabands . . . and selling them to parties who run them South." These suspicions were confirmed by the testimony of one man who reported to the provost marshal that he had been the victim of an attempted kidnapping. Two soldiers seized him while he was returning from market one day, bound and gagged him, and drove him some distance in a cart. They then "offered horse, cart, and man for three hundred dollars." When the soldiers retired to a bar for drinks, he managed to escape. As proof of his story, the victim's watch and some of his money were found on one of the soldiers. Although a reporter wrote that the men of the regiment felt "the utmost abhorrence of such barbarous and inhuman outrages," it is not known whether the kidnappers suffered any punishment.[23]

What motivated people to commit such a crime? Racism was a contributing factor. Had the rights of people of color been respected as much as those of whites, kidnapping could not have occurred, at least not to the extent that it did. As the free black population increased, so did racism and discrimination against blacks.[24] In 1790, slightly more than 27,000 free blacks lived in the North; by the time of the Civil War, this figure had increased tenfold, to nearly a quarter of a million.[25] Scholars of free black life such as Gary Nash have shown that whites felt threatened when the free black population of their area grew, and increased racism was often the result.[26]

Racism not only helped perpetuate the crime but also stalled prosecution. While abducting a white person usually resulted in action to rescue the victim and punish the kidnappers, the same crime committed against blacks met with apathy among most of the white community. This indifference was noticeable in the careless treatment that white newspaper reporters and letter writers often accorded black people. Sometimes the newspaper item identified a black only by first name, sometimes not even that. When names were given, little effort was made to standardize spelling. The cavalier attitude of most whites toward blacks made it possible for kidnappers to operate almost openly, with private citizens and government officials generally doing nothing to stop them.

At the root of the kidnapping of free blacks was the legality of slavery itself. The *African Observer* noted in 1827, "Where a traffic in slaves is thus actively carried on, and sanctioned by existing laws, those coloured persons who are legally free must necessarily hold their freedom by a very precarious tenure."[27] Slavery was supported by state laws, by the federal fugitive slave laws of 1793 and 1850, and by court cases such as *Prigg v. Pennsylvania* (1842), creating a climate that engendered kidnapping of free blacks. Although other laws existed to protect free blacks, they were only sporadically enforced and were not an effective counterweight to the laws that allowed for enslavement of free blacks. American law, beginning as early as the Constitution, generally served to protect slaveowners' property at the expense of black rights.

In the end, the primary motivation behind kidnapping was probably greed. Kidnapping free blacks and selling them into slavery could bring great financial reward. The prevailing motive of kidnappers was, as the Delaware Abolition Society termed it, "that fruitful source of evil—'the love of money.'"[28] According to abolitionist Edward Needles, the idea of making money in this fashion appealed to "the lower classes," as well as "some inferior magistrates and constables."[29] Free blacks, already vulnerable because of their race and socioeconomic disabilities, were further victimized by the profit motive. The prices that slaves generally brought were bolstered by the growth of cotton production after the invention of the cotton gin, by the close of the African slave trade, and by the expansion of slavery into the Southwest. By the 1850s, slave prices had soared, with good field hands usually bringing at least a thousand dollars and some artisans selling for more than twice that amount.[30] As long as the legal system and popular opinion tacitly permitted kidnapping and as long as slaves brought a good price on the market, there would be people unscrupulous enough to make money in this manner.

Some kidnappers of free blacks were members of professional gangs who often engaged in various other extralegal activities, particularly horse thieving and other forms of robbery. Others were average citizens who joined the ranks of kidnappers only when the opportunity to make money arose unexpectedly. Still other kidnappers were slave catchers who hunted fugitives for slaveowner clients. Slave catchers occasionally strayed beyond the law, accidentally or intentionally, by claiming free blacks as fugitives. As noted, not all kidnappers were white. Sometimes blacks worked with white abductors, often as lures. There is evidence that they worked alone as well.

One thing that kidnappers had in common, though, was the fear which they engendered in the black population, another element that made kidnapping possible. At the 1828 American Convention of Abolition Societies, Thomas Shipley, chair of the committee reporting on the internal slave trade, noted, "Individuals are well known, who have decoyed free people of color on board their vessels, . . . selling them as slaves." [31] Two Kentucky kidnappers, when arrested, threatened to "burn the city of Frankfort for interrupting their business." [32] The impunity with which kidnappers acted indicates that blacks were not alone in their fear of the criminals. It was common in some parts of the country for kidnapping to be practiced openly, without interference from authorities or from neighbors who feared retribution if they spoke out. Even those who were horrified at the kidnapping of free blacks into slavery were generally unwilling to endanger their own lives by assisting a person of color. As a result, many kidnappers escaped prosecution. Slaveowner-turned-abolitionist James G. Birney wrote in 1842, "No grand inquest has for years had the courage or virtue to find a bill of indictment against a kidnapper, however plain and undeniable the proof of his guilt." [33]

A case heard by the Pennsylvania Abolition Society (PAS) at a meeting in 1819 illustrates the barriers faced by a concerned citizen trying to assist a kidnapping victim. After he was informed that a free black girl, Sarah Hagerman, had been abducted and sold as a slave to Jesse Cannon of Norway's Fork Bridge, Maryland, John H. Willits traveled there to rescue her. Maryland sheriff John Brown said he wanted to assist Willits, but explained that since Cannon in fact lived across the state line, in Delaware, the matter was out of his jurisdiction. He offered, however, the name of Maryland Abolition Society member Anthony Wheatley, who knew Cannon well, having rescued blacks from him in the past.[34]

Willits met Wheatley, who told him that Jesse Cannon was "a notorious offender" who concealed and traded in stolen blacks. Wheatley advised Willits to seek help from Cannon's neighbor, Hatfield Wright, who advised Willits first to determine whether or not Sarah Hagerman was actually on the premises. "An agent" was found who, for five dollars, went to Cannon's house and reported that the girl was indeed there.[35] Willits and Wright then obtained a search warrant from the magistrate of Sussex County, Delaware. Seeking a constable to serve the warrant, Willits traveled to the town of Bridgeville at night, in a violent downpour. He went to the home of an abolitionist, a Dr. Carey, who told him that the only available constable was fifteen miles away in Georgetown. There Willits found the officer, who said he was going to be in court for several days. He directed Willits to another officer, who agreed to assist in serving the warrant. Both officers, however, Willits reported to the Pennsylvania Abolition Society, "expressed much apprehension at the violence which we should probably have to encounter, as it was believed that [Joe] Johnson, a son-in-law of Cannon's, was then at this house and him they represented as a most desparate ruffian guilty of a variety of crimes."[36]

Undaunted by this series of obstacles, Willits returned to Bridgeville with the constable, and with difficulty they recruited two men to join them. The group split up, two approaching Cannon's house from the front, two from the back. At the door, they encountered several small black girls, but not Sarah Hagerman. Joe Johnson brandished a pistol from the house, warning the men that their warrant had expired at sunset and that he would shoot them if they attempted to enter the house. The constable bravely replied that they had reached the house before dark and intended to search it. Johnson relented, but warned them not to ask any questions of the blacks inside. He and Jesse Cannon, both armed, followed the constable and Willits as they conducted the inspection.[37]

In a large garret, strongly barred, they discovered five young black women chained together. Hagerman was not among them. A small hut was also examined, but in it were only two black men, who were "much intoxicated and seemed quite happy." The group, Willits concluded in his report to the PAS, was forced to abandon its search for Sarah Hagerman, leaving her to an unknown fate.[38]

This incident illustrates the frustrating hurdles often encountered by those who attempted to free victims of illegal enslavement, including the fear generated by some kidnappers. Who were these men who frightened even the police? Both Jesse Cannon and Joe Johnson, the latter described by the Delaware attorney general as "perhaps the most celebrated kidnapper and negro stealer in the country," belonged to what was probably the most nefarious and successful kidnapping ring of the pre-Civil War era.[39] Evidence has suggested that the gang's real leader was Patty Cannon, Jesse's wife and Joe's mother-in-law. Whether or not she was the gang's mastermind, she certainly ranked among its most active and feared members. The organization and activities of the Cannon-Johnson gang indicate the ways in which many kidnappers operated to enslave free blacks.

The legend of Patty Cannon is well-known throughout Delaware and Maryland. Numerous accounts of her life exist, some of them outright fiction, others a mixture of fact and fable. Cannon has been the subject of several books, including George Alfred Townshend's *The Entailed Hat* (1884), R.W.

Messenger's *Patty Cannon Administers Justice* (1926), and Ted Giles's *Patty Cannon: Woman of Mystery* (1965). Most of the books, as well as newspaper and magazine articles about her, use as their major source a pamphlet published in 1841, *Narrative and Confessions of Lucretia P. Cannon.* Although the author is unknown, and there is some doubt as to the veracity of the work, some of the story it tells is certainly true.[40] Patty Hanley (her name before marriage), was described in the *Narrative* as "an uncommonly agreeable person and by no means bad-looking, though rather large. She was extravagantly fond of music, and dancing, a great talker, very witty and fascinating in her conversation, and concealing her real character so well that [her future husband, Alonzo Cannon, a wheelwright from Lower Delaware] . . . soon fell in love with her." This is an unusual depiction of a woman who died in a Delaware prison in 1829 while awaiting trial for several murders, including that of a baby she killed by throwing it into a fire.[41]

Long before this, however, abolitionists, local authorities, and many residents of the mid–Atlantic coast were aware of the extensive operations of Patty Cannon and her gang. In 1815, more than a decade prior to Cannon's death, John Kollock, constable of Georgetown, Delaware, wrote to the Pennsylvania Abolition Society to inform it of the gang's activities and associates. He referred specifically to Solomon Campbell and Jesse Leal of Philadelphia or Salem, New Jersey, who used a small sloop called *Two Brothers of Salem* to "fetch" blacks to sell as slaves in Carolina. They belonged to "a train of negro buyers" that included Jesse Cannon. Constable Kollock, helped by another man, had rescued two Philadelphia boys from Campbell and Leal. The boys, Richard Phillips and John Williams, said Campbell had enticed them on board a ship with the promise of peaches but had instead tried to sell them at a tavern in Delaware. Kollock returned the boys to their homes and received some financial compensation from the PAS.[42]

Early in 1816, the PAS discussed a report that placed Solomon Campbell in Philadelphia. The father of one of his victims per-

suaded the city's mayor to arrest the kidnapper. That summer, a grand jury brought two indictments against him, but
Campbell died before being brought to trial.[43]

Another case involving the Cannon-Johnson gang that
came to the attention of the Pennsylvania Abolition Society
was that of Abram Luomony, a young free black of Philadelphia, hired by Captain John Milner of the *Betsy* to sail
down the Delaware to Cohansey Creek, New Jersey, for
wood. At the mouth of the Broadkill River, Milner stopped
and sold Luomony. The victim, however, escaped and obtained assistance from abolitionists in Delaware, who sent
him back to Philadelphia with a letter detailing his circumstances. The mayor issued a warrant for Milner and William
Miller, who had aided in the kidnapping. Luomony testified
that as the sailboat had passed under a bridge spanning a small
creek, a man called Johnson jumped off the bridge onto the
boat. He and Miller tied and beat Luomony, robbed him of
five dollars and a knife, and took him to an old house in the
woods. There Johnson paid Miller, then took his captive by
carriage to Jesse Cannon's in Sussex County. After remaining
chained there for three days, Luomony managed to escape.
Miller's statement claimed that when the boat neared the
bridge, Luomony jumped ship, saying that he couldn't endure
the mosquitoes and was going to work in Milford. Milner
agreed that the black man had run away. The testimony of the
two, however, was not credible, for the mayor had them
jailed, and they were indicted by a grand jury for kidnapping.
At the trial, Luomony testified against them "in a very plain
and interesting manner," and as a result Miller was sentenced
to one year of hard labor and fined one hundred pounds.[44]

Several kidnappings brought the Cannon-Johnson ring
before the Circuit Court of the District of Columbia. In the
case of three blacks for whom a writ of habeas corpus was
sought, it was believed that they had been kidnapped and,
although free, were about to be sold as slaves. One was John
Parker, who said he had been abducted near Georgetown,
Delaware, by Jesse Cannon. Cannon had sold Parker to Will-

iam Palmer, who in turn sold him again. It appears that Palmer was an accomplice of Cannon's because another of the victims, Rosanna Brown, had been stolen from Middletown, Delaware, by Palmer and two other men. She was sold in Annapolis, Maryland. In 1816, Parker and Brown and her children successfully sued for their freedom. Their purchasers were not charged with kidnapping, as they had lost large sums of money in the transactions and appeared to have been unaware that the blacks had been kidnapped. Nor, apparently, was Jesse Cannon tried for the crime, although Palmer was indicted for kidnapping Rosanna Brown. Middletown lawyer John Reynolds told a colleague that he was happy "to find the unfortunate negro woman once more removed from the fangs of the Palmers and others, as vile a banditti as were ever permitted to disturb the peace of society."[45]

These cases represented only minor infractions of the law for the Cannon-Johnson gang. The extent of their activities was fully revealed in 1826 in a kidnapping case that involved some two dozen victims from Pennsylvania to Mississippi. These abductions brought notoriety to the gang when Philadelphia Mayor Joseph Watson made them his personal crusade. Evidence of the kidnappings first surfaced when Joe Johnson's brother Ebenezer stopped at the home of John Hamilton, a planter in Rocky Spring, Mississippi, and offered three boys and two women for sale. One of the boys told Hamilton that he and the others were not slaves but had been stolen from Philadelphia. Hamilton sent for a justice of the peace, who questioned Ebenezer Johnson. Johnson produced a bill of sale for the blacks, but agreed to let them remain at Hamilton's until this proof was verified. Johnson then left, supposedly to obtain further evidence of his ownership. Meanwhile, the alleged slaves told their stories to Hamilton.[46]

Samuel Scomp, at about age fifteen the oldest boy, was an indentured servant from Princeton, New Jersey, who had run away from his master. He went to Philadelphia, where a mulatto calling himself John Smith offered Scomp work unloading a ship. On board, Scomp encountered Joe Johnson, who tied Scomp's hands, put irons on his legs, and threatened to kill him with a knife if he made any noise.[47]

A second boy, Enos Tilman, about nine years old, told Hamilton that he had been an apprentice in Philadelphia when he was lured aboard the ship and chained by Smith. Another Philadelphian, Alexander Manlove, related a similar story. Mary Fisher, a free black woman from Delaware, explained that she had been gathering wood near the state border in Elkton, Maryland, when she was attacked by two men who took her to Joe Johnson's house. She said that a kidnapped boy called Joe had died on the journey to Mississippi. Another boy previously with them, Cornelius, had apparently been sold in Alabama. One woman among the group was a slave who had been legally purchased.[48]

In his letter to Philadelphia Mayor Joseph Watson, John Hamilton's lawyer, John Henderson (later U.S. senator from Mississippi), suggested that if the statements of these unfortunate blacks proved accurate, they should be published so that "the coloured people of your city and other places may be guarded against similar outrages." He added that he had no doubt as to Johnson's guilt. Henderson's belief was certainly correct, but he probably never imagined that he had helped uncover one of the largest mass kidnappings in American history.[49]

Apparently Watson followed Henderson's advice and publicized the incident, as the mayor received several letters in the next few months concerning the activities of the Cannon-Johnson gang. Delaware Attorney General James Rogers described his earlier attempts to bring the Johnson brothers to justice, and offered any information or assistance Watson requested.[50] Wilmington abolitionist Thomas Garrett provided information about one of the victims, known as Mary Fisher. He stated that he had read about the blacks' plight and believed the woman to be Charity Fisher, a Wilmington resident who had recently disappeared. Garrett added that he would continue to follow the case, and asked Watson to keep him apprised of any new developments.[51] Jesse Green, of

Concord, Delaware, wrote that Ebenezer Johnson had just returned from a slave-selling trip in Alabama and had resumed kidnapping blacks in the area.[52] James Bryan of Cambridge, Delaware, also offered information of the Johnsons and stated his belief that half of the suspected fugitive slaves on the peninsula were actually kidnapping victims taken by Johnson's "emissaries," who worked the field from Philadelphia to Accomak, Virginia. They numbered some thirty men, "as desperate as [Johnson]." Bryan also placed some of the blame on the Delaware legislature, which he claimed was more concerned with recovering runaways than with liberating kidnapped free blacks.[53]

As a result of the publicity given to the incident, the gang's black confederate, John Smith, was located. Georgetown, Delaware, resident Thomas Layton wrote to James Rogers informing him that Smith had been seen in the area and was using the alias Spencer Francis.[54] In response, a Philadelphia constable was sent to investigate.[55]

In Mississippi, John Hamilton had examined the documents relevant to the case, concluding that the slaves offered for sale by Ebenezer Johnson had in fact been kidnapped. Hamilton contacted Mississippi authorities. The state's attorney general, Richard Stockton, wrote to Mayor Watson at Hamilton's request, and notified him that everything was being done to effect the return of the victims to their homes and the prosecution of the kidnappers. Although Mississippi was a slave state, Stockton assured Watson, "There is no community that holds in greater abhorrence, that infamous traffic carried on by negro stealers." He added that no other state made it easier for those held illegally in slavery to gain their liberty.[56]

In June, a deposition was taken in the Philadelphia mayor's office from Samuel Scomp, who had returned to the city with some of the other blacks after spending several months at Hamilton's plantation. Scomp's statement confirmed and elaborated upon the account he had given to John Henderson in Mississippi. After John Smith had lured him on board a ship docked in Philadelphia, Scomp was secured in the hold with two other boys, Enos Tilman and Alexander Manlove. They said that they had been abducted the night before, also enticed aboard by Smith. Two more boys were brought to the ship later that day, Cornelius Sinclair and the ironically named Joe Johnson.[57]

That night the ship sailed. In a week, it landed near the kidnapper Johnson's house along the Delaware-Maryland border, where the captives were confined in an attic. They were later moved to the Cannon house and chained there for about a week. There, two women, Mary Fisher, a free woman from Delaware, and Maria Neal, a slave, joined them. The whole group was then transported by boat to the Deep South; Scomp was unsure exactly where they landed. The victims were forced to walk through Alabama, where several of them were sold. Cornelius Sinclair was the first to be sold, bringing four hundred dollars in Tuscaloosa. The rest were forced to walk on to Mississippi, where they finally stopped at Rocky Spring, site of John Hamilton's plantation. Scomp estimated that they had traveled about thirty miles each day on foot and had received a severe whipping if they complained. When he tried to escape, Scomp was beaten "with a hand saw and with hickories" by Ebenezer Johnson. The deposition noted that an examination of Scomp's back confirmed the beatings.[58]

About seven miles outside Rocky Spring, the boy called Joe Johnson died from the beatings and from frostbite of the feet. At Hamilton's, all but the slave Maria Neal were taken in and cared for. After several months, the planter obtained passage for them to New Orleans, from where they sailed to Philadelphia. Mary Fisher, who did not want to travel by sea, remained at Hamilton's.[59]

Philadelphia Mayor Joseph Watson kept the Pennsylvania Abolition Society informed of his ongoing investigation. In July, William Rawle, PAS president, received word from Watson that Ebenezer Johnson had been arrested for possessing the body of the boy who had died on the journey. Watson reported the return of most of the victims and added that

Cornelius Sinclair was expected to arrive shortly. The Grand Jury of Philadelphia County issued indictments against Ebenezer and Joe Johnson, John Smith, and Thomas Collins, another gang member. Warrants for their arrest were forwarded to Delaware, Maryland, Virginia, Alabama, and Mississippi. Watson also told the PAS that he had forwarded documents that supported the victims' statements.[60]

But the case did not end there, for the activities of the Johnson brothers exceeded the scope of the initial reports. In December 1826, evidence of another kidnapping by the gang surfaced. David Holmes, governor of Mississippi, and Joseph E. Davis, lawyer and state legislator of Natchez, notified Watson of the story of Peter Hook, a slave in Mississippi. In a deposition recorded by lawyer Duncan S. Walker, Hook revealed that he had been kidnapped in Philadelphia in June 1825[61] one night when a black man named John invited him to a ship near the Arch Street wharf for a drink. On board, Joe Johnson took him below, tied him up, and chained him to a pump. Two others, William Miller and Milton Trusty, were brought down the same night and chained with Hook. Clement Cox and William Chase, two more kidnapping victims, arrived the next night. After several days, the ship sailed, and eventually all the victims were taken to Joe Johnson's house, where they were shackled in the attic. Several more victims arrived over the next few days: John Jacobs, a cart driver, James Bayard, a sweep, Benjamin Baxter, "little Jack," Ephraim Lawrence, "little John," and Henry. All were boys except Henry, who was a young man.[62]

Two girls, Lydia Smith and Sarah (Sally) Nicholson, were chained in a different part of the attic. According to Hook, the entire group remained at Johnson's house for about six months and were then taken to Rockingham, North Carolina, and were sold. Hook reported that they were severely beaten when they asserted their free status. Two other black men, Staten and Constant, who said they had been abducted from Philadelphia, joined the group near Rockingham. Miller and Sutler, slave traders, purchased the blacks from Johnson and sold them at various points. Hook was sold to a man named Perryman in Holmesville, Mississippi, along with three of the other boys.[63]

In January 1827, Philadelphia Mayor Watson thanked David Holmes and J. E. Davis for the information they had added to the state's case against the Cannon-Johnson gang. He told them of the gang's other kidnappings and explained that he hoped "to develope the mazes of this infernal plot, by means of which, a great number of free born children, during several years past, have been seduced away and kidnapped, principally, and almost wholly as I believe, by a gang of desperadoes, whose haunts and head quarters are now known to have been, on the dividing line between the states of Delaware and Maryland, low down on the peninsula, between the Delaware and Chesapeake bays."

Warrants for the arrest of the Cannon-Johnson gang had been issued in several states.[64] Watson had found white witnesses who could identify three of the boys, although he recognized the difficulty of getting whites to testify to the identity of the blacks, especially after so much time had elapsed.[65] The city council of Philadelphia authorized the mayor to issue a five-hundred-dollar reward for information leading to the arrest and prosecution of anyone involved in the kidnappings of 1825. The council also provided five hundred dollars to the mayor for expenses incurred in the investigation.[66] This proclamation was issued to newspapers the following day.[67] Watson advised Duncan S. Walker, the Mississippi lawyer working to secure the freedom and safe return of the victims, "to leave no stone unturned" in his efforts to help the blacks. The Philadelphia mayor clearly followed the same policy himself.[68]

Walker brought freedom suits for five of the blacks. His brother Robert J. Walker, also an attorney, investigated the circumstances of the six whose whereabouts were unknown. Duncan Walker sympathized with Watson. "I can appreciate the difficulty you anticipate, of indentifying black children, by the evidence of white persons," he wrote. "But however onerous it may be on all hands, we must do our duty." It seemed surprising that Walker, a southerner, would expend so much effort to assist people of color. Yet he was sincere: he refused any fees for his services, despite Watson's offer of compensation, and he assured the mayor, "Our soil affords no stone for building Penitentiaries, but our forests supply gallows for the kidnapper; while our laws protect slave property, they will restore the free."[69] Walker also sent the statement of another of the victims, Lydia Smith of Delaware. An indentured servant, she had been shunted among numerous masters for many of her twenty-three years. Her last master, Bill Spicer, had been jailed for attempting to sell her as a slave. When he was released, he sold Smith to Ebenezer Johnson for $110. Chained for about five months in the home of Johnson's sister, Smith there encountered Ephraim Lawrence, John Jacobs, and little John. They were eventually taken to Rockingham, North Carolina.[70]

Watson then asked James Rogers, attorney general of Delaware, if he could "obtain depositions as to the general infamous character of these kidnappers."[71] The Philadelphia grand jury would be sitting in March, and Watson believed that the Johnsons would be indicted for kidnapping. He planned to ask Pennsylvania Governor John Schultze to demand the Johnson's extradition from Mississippi and to make arrangements for the children's return. Watson had no doubt that they had all been kidnapped.[72] In fact, he believed that most of the kidnappings that had occurred over the past ten years in the mid–Atlantic region were the work of the Johnson brothers, whom he characterized as "very desperate ruffians, and utterly infamous."[73]

The Cannon-Johnson family managed to avoid apprehension, however. As Delawarian Jesse Green reported in March 1827, the Johnson brothers had returned to Patty Cannon's home in Delaware and planned to resume their kidnapping operation, with blacks "to assist and decoy." Stating that "the poor Free Negroes feel much alarm at their return," Green added that while he would continue to provide authorities with any information he could, he was too old to offer any other help. He also wanted his name kept secret for fear of the gang's revenge.[74]

That same month, a Natchez, Mississippi, newspaper editorial spoke out against the kidnappings: "Policy, as well as humanity, requires that our citizens take every measure in their power to assist in restoring these unfortunate beings to their homes, and their families." Despite the tone of most of the editorial, however, it claimed that "for the most part free negroes are the worst description of people that could ever be willingly brought among us."[75] The extensive laws passed by Mississippi and other southern states reveal an intensive attempt to prevent free blacks from entering their borders and to control the existing black population. Perhaps the efforts of southern citizens to return the victims of the Cannon–Johnson gang to their homes were an indication, not of sympathy for fellow human beings in trouble, nor of obedience to antikidnapping laws, but of the desire to expunge a group of people whom they viewed with distaste and fear.

Southerners nonetheless played an important role in restoring kidnapped free blacks to their northern homes. Joshua Boucher of Tuscaloosa, for example, labored to secure the release of Cornelius Sinclair, who had been sold by the Johnsons to James Paul of Tuscaloosa and who was suing for his freedom.[76] Early in 1827, Boucher informed Watson that Sinclair had been declared free by the court, "which has afforded not a little pleasure to many of the benevolent of this place." Boucher wanted to bring to Watson's attention the case of another Philadelphia boy held illegally by Joe Johnson: Jacob Simon, called Charly, enslaved in an adjoining Alabama county. He had been abducted in Philadelphia in April 1825, and taken south by Johnson. Boucher offered his help with any future kidnapping cases.[77]

Residents of the Upper South were also working to gain the blacks' freedom. Delaware abolitionist Thomas Garrett, who had become involved in the case as soon as he had knowledge of it, provided proof of the free status of another victim, Sarah Nicholson. Nicholson's case was especially poignant, as Garrett summed up: "Her eyesight is nearly gone, and . . . she can be of but little value to her master and perhaps he would be glad to get rid of her, if he could do it without involving him in further expense."[78]

Watson sent Philadelphia constable Samuel Garrigues to Louisiana, where he secured the liberty of two other boys taken by the gang, Clement Cox and Ephraim Lawrence, and promised that Sarah Nicholson would soon follow. However, difficulties were encountered in the other cases in obtaining "strictly legal proof—that is to say, the evidence of white persons in open court."[79] This was a common problem. Even though there were witnesses to the crime, many kidnapping cases were lost in court because of the inadmissability of black testimony in cases involving whites. Even when white witnesses were available, they were frequently reluctant to testify. Fear of retribution and racism prevented many whites from testifying in cases of kidnapping, which usually involved a black plaintiff and white defendant.

Ironically, when members of the Cannon-Johnson kidnapping ring were finally brought to justice, it was not for the crime of kidnapping. In fact, few of the gang were ever convicted of that offense. Joe Johnson was first charged with forcibly taking a free black person into Maryland in 1817. Several others were charged as well, including Johnson's father-in-law, Jesse Cannon, and Cannon's son, Jesse, Jr., but only Johnson was tried. In 1822, he was found guilty by a Delaware court and sentenced to a public whipping—thirty-nine lashes "well laid on." In addition, Johnson was ordered to stand in the pillory for one hour with both ears nailed to it, then to "have the soft part of both his ears cut off." The sheriff reported to the court that Johnson's sentence had been "inflicted agreeably to the order of the court," except for the order to cut off his ears, which had been remitted by the governor.[80]

At about the same time, Johnson escaped numerous other attempts to make him pay for his crimes. In 1821, he was found not guilty in three other cases of kidnapping and false imprisonment. In these cases, other gang members had also been charged but were not brought to trial. On another charge of kidnapping and assault and battery in 1822, Johnson again was found not guilty.[81]

Since most of the Cannon-Johnson gang paid nothing for their crimes of kidnapping, and since Joe Johnson was found innocent more times than not, the family's brushes with the law did not deter them from their illegal activities. When they were finally halted by authorities, in fact, it was not for the crime of kidnapping, rather for murder. "Shocking Depravity," declared the *Delaware Gazette and American Watchman* of April 10, 1829, which printed a letter from a Sussex County reader who revealed "a shocking course of murderous deeds" that had been going on for some time along the Delaware-Maryland border. A tenant farmer on Patty Cannon's farm in North West Fork Hundred discovered a chest buried in the ground that contained human bones. News spread quickly, and neighbors recalled the suspicious disappearance of a man in the area.[82]

Cyrus James, a member of the gang who had been reared by the Cannon family since age seven, was taken in for questioning by the magistrate at Seaford. He claimed that while he was living at Patty Cannon's about ten or twelve years earlier, she, Joe, and Ebenezer Johnson had murdered a Georgia slave trader named Bell or Miller who was having supper at Cannon's house. She and the Johnson brothers had shot and robbed him and buried his body in the trunk that was later unearthed. This was not the first murder they had committed, the witness declared, and he took the police to other places where bodies were uncovered. One was the body of a black child of a woman owned by the Cannons; the child had been killed because Patty Cannon believed the father was a member of the Cannon-Johnson family. Two oak boxes were also unearthed; one of them held what were believed to be the bones of a seven-year-old child Cannon had killed by striking its head with a piece of wood.[83]

With these charges against her, Patty Cannon was apprehended and lodged in the Georgetown, Delaware, jail, but the Johnson brothers could not be located. Joe had last been seen in Delaware during the winter, but he was later forced to flee the area because of his growing notoriety and the price that Philadelphia Mayor Watson had placed on his head. He was said to have gone to Alabama, while his brother Ebenezer had fled to Mississippi.[84]

In April 1829, the Grand Jury of Sussex County, Delaware, returned three indictments against Patty Cannon for murder. "Not having the fear of God before her eyes, but being moved and seduced by the instigation of the Devil," Cannon was charged with assaulting an infant female in 1822, strangling and suffocating it and causing the infant's death "willingly and with malice aforethought."[85] This may be the incident recounted in the *Narrative* when the crying of a five-year-old girl so annoyed Cannon that she beat the child, then held her face in the fire and burned her to death.[86] The grand jury also indicted Patty Cannon for the murders of two other children.[87]

In October 1829, Patty Cannon and the Johnson brothers were tried in absentia. Patty Cannon was charged with the murders of three children, Joe Johnson with participating in two of them, Ebenezer Johnson with complicity in one.[88] Elusive to the end, none of the gang was present for the trial. Patty Cannon had died in jail on May 11, 1829, and the Johnsons were apparently never found. According to the *Narrative*, all were convicted and sentenced to be hanged. Three other gang members were convicted as accessories and sentenced to seven years in prison: four years of hard labor and three of solitary confinement each. In jail awaiting trial, Cannon had managed to obtain poison, and she died "a most terrible and awful death." Before she died, however, she called in a priest and confessed to the murder of eleven people, admitting that she had been an accomplice in at least twelve others. Among the deaths that Cannon acknowledged responsibility for were those of her husband, whom she had poisoned, and one of her own children, whom she had strangled three days after it was born.[89]

Interestingly, the only member of the Cannon-Johnson

gang who was convicted of kidnapping, other than Joe Johnson, was the black kidnapper John Purnell (alias John Smith, Spencer Francis, James Morris). It was Purnell who had performed most of the initial abductions for the gang's mass kidnapping of 1825. He had been indicted for two kidnappings in Delaware in 1821, apparently escaping conviction at that time,[90] but the law finally caught up with him.

Captured in the summer of 1827 in Boston by Samuel Garrigues, the Philadelphia constable, Purnell was returned to face charges of kidnapping blacks from Philadelphia and selling them south.[91] Several witnesses testified, apparently before the Philadelphia grand jury, to Purnell's involvement in kidnapping schemes. Simon Wesley Parker, a black, stated that he had first become acquainted with Purnell several years before. One day, Parker encountered Purnell in a Philadelphia oyster shop with a young boy. Purnell and the boy left, and then Purnell returned alone and warned Parker that if he said anything about the boy, Purnell "would blow his [Parker's] brains out." After Purnell left again, the shop owner, Henry Carr, told Parker that Purnell intended to take the boy on board a ship and sell him as a slave. The ship's captain then appeared at the shop, and Carr addressed him as Captain Moore. But Carr told Parker later that the man had several aliases and was in fact "the notorious Joe Johnson." Carr and Parker went with Johnson to the ship, where Johnson told Carr, "I want you to fetch me one or two more by twelve o'clock." He gave Carr twenty-five dollars, and Carr and Parker went in search of boys to be abducted on South Street. There they encountered Purnell, who took half the money as payment for the victims he had already delivered. The next day, Purnell told Parker that Carr had been cheating him and asked if Parker wanted to be his accomplice. According to his testimony, Parker believed the kidnapped boy was Jacob [Simon], the Philadelphia boy enslaved in Alabama mentioned by Joshua Boucher in his letter to Mayor Watson.[92]

Cornelius Sinclair, one of the rescued kidnapping victims, also testified at the hearing, recounting how Purnell had picked him up on the street, placed a "sticking plaster" on his mouth to prevent him from crying out, and put him into a cart that he drove toward the navy yard. He was then taken aboard Johnson's ship, where he encountered other captives, Samuel Scomp, Enos Tilman, Alexander Manlove, and later "Joe the sweep." After a journey by ship, the boys were tied and transported in a wagon to a house where they were chained in an attic.[93]

Purnell had lured Samuel Scomp to the ship by asking for his help in loading watermelons. Scomp "considered it a marvelously good joke at being decoyed in this manner. [He] laughed at the recollection of the treatment he had received, and the audience laughed with him." Tilman had been decoyed by Purnell in a similar way, while Purnell had abducted Manlove while the boy slept on Market Street. Both John Purnell and Henry Carr were indicted for kidnapping, and there was some consideration of charging Purnell in federal court for piracy.[94] Purnell, found guilty on two counts of kidnapping in the 1827 trial, was sentenced to the full measure of the law—four thousand dollars and forty-two years in prison.[95] As the *Niles Register* reported, "This fellow's kidnapping days are over."[96]

Three years earlier the same paper had announced the death of Purnell. In 1824, it reported that three slaves employed by Purnell as kidnappers had beaten one of their victims to death when he tried to escape. They showed the body to Purnell, then threw it in the river. After the three slaves were taken into custody and confessed, the police began hunting for Purnell. When his capture was imminent, he cut his throat "from ear to ear" and died instantly, the paper had reported, stating that he was suspected of kidnapping hundreds of people.[97] It is unlikely, however, that there were two black kidnappers named Purnell operating in Maryland in the 1820s, and a black of that name was known to have been with the Cannon-Johnson gang after 1824. It appears, then, that either the newspaper report was a case of mistaken identity or Purnell survived his attempted suicide.

Another case involving the gang surfaced after Patty Cannon died in jail, and it may have included John Purnell. The *Delaware Gazette* reported the gang's use of black accomplices to lure victims, and noted that one in particular was an expert at this practice. Purnell certainly fit this description, and since the article recounted a past incident for which no date was given, it could have occurred prior to Purnell's incarceration. Another black kidnapper furnished the details of this heartrending case of kidnapping. On one occasion, the black man working for the gang encountered a Maryland slave who had a free wife and seven sons, ages six to eighteen. The kidnapper persuaded the slave to go with him to Camden, Delaware, under the pretense of obtaining a pass from the Quakers that would get him to New Jersey. The slave was taken to Patty Cannon's house, provided with a fake document, then permitted to leave. The kidnapper told the man's family that he had escaped to freedom and offered to take them to join their father in New Jersey. The family was never seen or heard from again.[98]

A variety of circumstances prevented authorities from quickly capturing and prosecuting the members of the Cannon-Johnson gang. Certainly detection of their crimes was not a problem. As shown by the evidence presented above, state and local authorities, abolitionists, and private citizens in several areas were well aware of the gang's kidnapping operations. But knowledge of the gang's activities included knowledge of the violence with which they intimidated both their captives and those who tried to interfere with their illegal acts. Many chose silence.

Greed played a part as well. Kidnapping was a lucrative business, lucrative enough to draw even blacks into the practice of selling fellow blacks into slavery. There is some evidence that avarice was one of the government's motivations for ignoring the problem. Part of the legend surrounding Patty Cannon held that she bribed local sheriffs to prevent them from investigating her affairs.[99]

The Cannon-Johnson gang was fortunate in the location of its headquarters, on the Eastern Shore, within traveling distance of Philadelphia, which gave the gang access to a large free black population. The siting of the family's homes was also crucial to both its kidnapping operations and the avoidance of capture. Two homes, within "calling distance" of one another, were located in a heavily wooded section along the southern border of Delaware and Maryland. Far from any towns, the homes were situated near the Nanticoke River, which empties into the Chesapeake Bay, enabling the gang to operate by water as well as by land. [100]

The location not only expedited kidnapping, but also rendered capture of the gang problematic. "Patty's house was erected squarely on the line between the two states, so that when officers from one state came for her she had but to go into an adjoining room to be out of their jurisdiction." [101] The Cannon home rested not only in two states, but in three counties as well—Sussex County in Delaware and Dorchester and Caroline counties in Maryland. [102]

Though not as common as white kidnappers, more than a few blacks were active in the business of kidnapping. The best known and probably the most successful was John Purnell, who illustrated the advantage that being black gave to a kidnapper. As a black, he was able to gain the trust of others of his race, even those alert to the dangers of kidnapping. For this reason, most black kidnappers decoyed their victims, rather than using the forcible abduction commonly employed by whites.

Like Purnell, some other black kidnappers worked in concert with whites. In 1860, a black man from Cincinnati was arrested along with his white partner, a blind South Carolinian, for kidnapping and attempting to sell a free black in Memphis. [103] Others worked alone. The records of the Pennsylvania Abolition Society note the arrest of black kidnapper Absalom Cork. In Philadelphia, Cork had abducted two free blacks, one of them his own cousin. He sold both in the South, but they escaped and returned to Philadelphia to press charges. [104]

Just as the practice of kidnapping knew no racial boundaries, it was also not bounded by sex. A black woman, Emily Medal, was taken into police custody on the charge of kidnapping a seven-year-old boy from the Colored Orphan Asylum in Cincinnati. Although she claimed that she was his legal guardian, a warrant was issued on an affadavit by abolitionist Levi Coffin, and a marshal went to New Richmond, Ohio, to arrest Medal and recover the boy. The officer found her at home, but while he waited in another room for her to get ready to leave with him, Medal escaped through a trap door leading to an underground passage. Although she had fifteen minutes' head start, the officer caught her and took her into custody. [105]

Another black female kidnapper was known as Tilly. In 1824, Isaiah Sadler testified before Philadelphia Mayor Joseph Watson that Tilly, with several male accomplices, had attempted to kidnap him. Sadler related that he had been traveling with Tilly when they stopped overnight at a tavern. Sadler grew suspicious of the men in the tavern, but his companion reassured him. The next morning, one of the men accused them of being fugitives; two men chained Sadler to a tree in the woods by means of a padlock. Later taken to another house, he was told that Tilly had proven her freedom and was released. But a black woman in the house told Sadler that Tilly was actually part of the gang. Sadler managed to escape and in Milford, Delaware, received help from a group of Quakers, who sent him by ship to Philadelphia. [106]

Although it is difficult enough to comprehend the actions of any kidnappers, it is perhaps most difficult to fathom the motivation of the blacks among them. But knowing that money was the major motive for kidnapping perhaps makes it easier to understand the behavior of black kidnappers, who may have turned to crime as a means of surviving.

The examples of black kidnappers notwithstanding, blacks were the targets far more frequently than they were the instigators of kidnapping activity, and blacks were involved more often in resisting abduction than in participating in the activity. In both kidnapping and resisting kidnapping, blacks acted sometimes in concert with whites, sometimes alone.

One thing shared by all kidnappers was the illegal nature of their activity. Some kidnappers, however, managed not only to evade the law, but even to turn it to their advantage. While kidnapping was illegal in nearly all states, other laws inadvertently facilitated the sale of free blacks into slavery. The intersection of these two types of laws, the subject of the next chapter, helps to illuminate the precarious legal status of free blacks in the United States before the Civil War.

CHAPTER TWO

"The Legitimate Offspring of Slavery": Kidnappers Who Operated within the Law

The forceful abduction of free blacks for sale into slavery was illegal in all states before the Civil War. However, the prac-tice of enslaving free people of color was also achieved by legal means. Particularly vulnerable in this regard were free blacks claimed as fugitives. Because blacks claimed as runaways were denied due process under the fugitive slave laws of 1793 and 1850, the potential for enslavement of legally free people was great.

The federal fugitive slave laws were well-known and protested by many, but numerous lesser-known laws also rendered black freedom precarious. Most southern states, for example, enacted laws restricting—in some cases even prohibiting—the manumission of slaves. These laws were designed to keep in bondage those who were legally enslaved, but even slaves who had been legally manumitted by their owners could be reenslaved under certain conditions. Heirs successfully challenged wills in which slaveowners had freed their slaves. Emancipated slaves could be returned to bondage in payment of their former masters' debts, and manumitted slaves would lose their freedom if they did not leave their home state within a certain time period.

Free blacks might also be enslaved for the simple act of entering most southern states. Many western territories also had such laws; even northern state legislatures debated their passage. Free black sailors faced a similar predicament. As free blacks, they could not legally enter southern states, yet a great number of the ships trading in southern ports employed black seamen. Southern state governments dealt with this problem by ordering the imprisonment of black sailors while their ships were docked. If captains did not pay the jail fees, black sailors could be sold into slavery. Actually any free black, once jailed, was liable to enslavement to pay jail fees. Sailors, unclaimed suspected fugitives, and even debtors, therefore, could be legally enslaved because of lack of money.

All of these laws were part of a large body of "black codes" designed by southern states to control and suppress their black populations, free and slave. Free blacks, in particular, were viewed with fear, suspicion, and hatred by southern whites. Slaves, at least, posed no legal difficulties because they were property, with few rights beyond slaveowners' obligation to feed and clothe them and the prohibition of the willful infliction of death. Free blacks, however, existed in legal limbo, neither slave nor citizen. The uncertainty of their status presented a constant danger in the eyes of the southern white population. Especially after the 1822 rebellion in Charleston, South Carolina, led by free black artisan Denmark Vesey, southern whites increasingly feared that the mere existence of a free black class posed a threat to the stability of southern society. The majority of free blacks were not active abolitionists, stirring up slave resentment and discontent. But their very existence represented a condition of black life that contradicted slave status and, therefore, could provide a temptation to all slaves. Thus some southern states tried to eliminate their free black populations, while others attempted at least to severely constrain them.[1]

Under the Fugitive Slave Law of 1793, slaveowners and their agents were permitted to enter free states, seize fugitive slaves, and after obtaining certification from a magistrate, return home with their property.[2] Suspected slaves were thus denied due process of law.[3] Not only did the 1793 law facilitate the return of escaped slaves, it was also, as Don E. Fehrenbacher has termed it, "an invitation to kidnapping, whether the result of honest error or deliberate fraud,"[4]

Like its predecessor, the Fugitive Slave Law of 1850 authorized slaveholders and their agents to seize blacks without due process,[5] and several features of the later law actually made the practice of kidnapping easier. Special federal commissioners were appointed to hear fugitive slave cases, enabling southern slaveowners to bypass northern state officials.[6] These commissioners earned five dollars for each case in which a suspect was set free, ten dollars for each person remanded to slavery.[7] And where there was reason to believe abolitionists might stage a rescue attempt, a suspected fugitive could be taken into a southern state without a warrant issued by the commissioner.[8] According to David Potter, "The law left all free Negroes with inadequate safeguards against claims that they were fugitives, and it exposed them to the danger of kidnapping." Potter argued, "For years this danger of being dragged away into slavery had made the life of the free Negro precarious, and it was undoubtedly accentuated by the new law."[9]

Sometimes a free person was taken into slavery by mistake. Such was perhaps the case with the seizure of James Valentine. In July of 1860, less than a year before the firing on Fort Sumter, agents of Georgetown (District of Columbia) slaveowner Joshua Bateman came to Philadelphia in search of the fugitive slave Ben Hurd. After obtaining a warrant from a Philadelphia judge, they set off in pursuit of Hurd. Assuming that he had gotten a job as a waiter in one of the city's hotels, the three agents, accompanied by two deputy marshals, had no luck until they spotted a black man driving a wagon filled with dry goods. Claiming he was Hurd, they seized the driver, handcuffed him, and took him to the marshal's office. Noticing the commotion, a crowd collected, and several of the people told the officers that a mistake had been made, that the man they had arrested was a longtime resident of Philadelphia. The agents then admitted that he was not Hurd. James Valentine, born free in Salem, New Jersey, and a resident of Philadelphia since 1826, planned to bring suit against the marshals for assault. Whether he did so is not known.[10]

Black travelers, especially, were in danger of being abducted and sold as fugitives. In its 1831 "Address to the Free People of the United States," the *Liberator* noted, "In traveling through the slave states, they [blacks] are liable to be taken up, in every town and district, on suspicion as runaway slaves, thrust into prison, confined sixty days or more, and sometimes sold into bondage for their jail fees."[11] Thomas Parsons, a free black resident of Monongalia County in western Virginia, knew firsthand the validity of this warning. In October of 1837, he set out for the Northwest Territory. Later that year, a letter arrived at the Knottsville post office in Monongalia County stating that Parsons had been jailed in Mayslick, Kentucky, as a fugitive. Court officers of Monongalia County notified Kentucky authorities that Parsons was in fact free and should be allowed to leave. The record does not reveal whether Parsons was actually released.[12]

Another unfortunate traveler, Lunsford Lane, was arrested in Baltimore with his companion, John Jones. The two former slaves supposedly answered the descriptions of two fugitives from North Carolina. Both men had free papers, letters of introduction, and permits to travel on the railroad, which they were afraid to surrender. In fact both men were former slaves of North Carolina governors. After gaining his freedom, Jones, a tailor, settled in Illinois, where he and his wife Mary ran an Underground Railroad station. Lane had worked at a number of occupations (including abolitionist lecturer) while traveling along the northeastern seaboard raising money to purchase his family from slavery.[13]

When the first case (Jones's) went to court, the judge claimed that free papers could be forged. Moreover, Lane's testimony that Jones was free was not sufficient proof because Lane was black. The lawyer for the two men argued that no evidence existed to show that Jones was a slave. When the slave catchers refused to show their documents including the descriptions of the runaways, the defendants' lawyer launched into an impassioned discourse on the subject of kidnapping. He declared that it "had now become so common that a free colored man found it almost impossible to pass safely from one State to another." The judge dismissed the case.[14]

Lane's plight was a particularly apt case because he had had a similar brush with the law earlier. After purchasing his freedom, he had left his home in North Carolina to work in New York to earn money to purchase his family's freedom. When he returned home, he was arrested under a state law prohibiting free black immigration. After authorities released him, a mob confronted Lane and examined his possessions in search of abolitionist literature. With surprising good humor, Lane recounted how they discovered his bag held only "a pair of old shoes, and a pair of old boots!—but they did not conclude that these were incendiary." Several men, still not satisfied, tarred and feathered Lane later that evening. Eventually, however, he managed to purchase his family and moved with them to Philadelphia.[15]

While their adversaries perhaps genuinely mistook Lane and Jones for runaways, others used the federal fugitive slave laws to seize people they had no reason to believe were slaves, sometimes even those known to be free. This was apparently the case with C. W. Jones, a Kansas resident. One night four men stopped at Jones's home. While he helped them with their horses and wagon, they seized and beat him and ordered him to disclose his owner's name. Jones had never been a slave and in fact three of his great-grandfathers had been white. Yet he was taken to the St. Joseph jail, where authorities later released him in acknowledgment that he was not a fugitive slave. Jones went to Quindaro and filed charges against Deputy U.S. Marshal Louis Cox and Samuel Forsyth, sheriff of Wyandotte County. Their defense attorney, A.C. Davis, charged Jones with counterfeiting and brought in two witnesses against him. These witnesses turned out to be two of Jones's kidnappers, both of whom fled the court, one even before testifying. They were pursued by an officer with a writ of kidnapping, but escaped his jurisdiction by going to Kansas City, Missouri. In the absence of the witnesses against Jones, he was then released. A local reporter concluded, "There exists in [Kansas City], and in various parts of the Kansas Territory, a large and dangerous band of men—many of them holding high positions in the community—who are banded together for the purpose of kidnapping free men, and selling them into slavery." [16]

The vulnerability of free black people was so extreme that even those who could prove their free status might fail to receive legal protection and might even become victims of the law. A free black mistakenly jailed as a fugitive could end up a slave even after his or her free status had been established. Numerous state laws fostered situations that led to the eventual enslavement of legally free people. In most southern states, blacks who were jailed for any reason could be legally sold into slavery to pay their jail and court fees. Thus, if a black were jailed as a fugitive and no one claimed ownership of the suspect and paid the jail fees, then he or she could, ironically, be sold into slavery. This was the experience of James Waggoner, a free black of Cincinnati, who was taken by two men and jailed as a fugitive in Newport, Kentucky. Although no one claimed Waggoner, he could not prove his free status to the satisfaction of the authorities, so he remained in jail for six months. Unable to pay his fees, Waggoner was then sold to a Newport man, who sent him to Lexington to be sold again. In a second cruel injustice, his abductors were lodged in the same jail after they were apprehended for kidnapping him. Since it was only the word of Waggoner, a black man, against theirs, they were released. Ultimately, however, Waggoner managed to sue successfully in circuit court for his freedom. [17]

Many other victims of similar circumstance could be found in the advertisements for sales of unclaimed fugitives in southern newspapers. The Washington, D.C., *National Intelligencer* carried a notice, for example, requesting that the owner of Polly Seiper and her infant son claim them. Committed as a fugitive, Polly claimed to have been manumitted in 1828 by her master, John Campbell of Virginia. Nevertheless, she and her child were to be sold for jail fees as the law directed if no one claimed them. [18]

Free blacks incarcerated for reasons other than suspicion of being runaways faced similar difficulties. Even if eventually found innocent of the crime of which they were charged, free blacks could become enslaved if they failed to pay their fees. The majority of the black population often found payment of fees impossible.

A tragic example of this dilemma occurred in Goldsboro, North Carolina, in 1852 when a free black named Wynne lost his wife and children, sold into slavery because he had fallen into debt. He himself had purchased his wife's freedom from slavery. She and their children were, nonetheless, considered his personal property, so they were sold to pay his debts.[19]

In addition to the utter disregard for black rights, the growing controversy over states' rights versus federal power acted to reinforce antiblack laws. Although the concept of states' rights has usually been associated with southern efforts to protect slavery, both northerners and southerners employed the states' rights argument in the case of kidnapping. Southerners enacted laws in violation of the Constitution, such as those that allowed the imprisonment of black sailors who had committed no crime, while at the same time they resented what they perceived as northern attemps to deprive them of their slaves. But in the case of kidnapping, it was the northern states that protested federal restrictions, in the form of fugitive slave laws. Mirroring southern behavior, several northern states enacted personal liberty laws designed to protect northern interests. Northerners believed the federal government was pro-southern because it gave southern slaveowners and their agents free rein both to retrieve fugitive slaves who had escaped to the North and to kidnap northern free blacks. Personal liberty laws prohibited northern authorities from assisting in fugitive recapture.[20] The fact that both southern and northern states began to enact more legislation concerning blacks after the 1830s is a reflection of the growing sectional controversy.

But sectional controversy over slavery predated this antebellum agitation. It was sectional controversy that turned the attempt to gain redress for a kidnapped free black into the passage of the nation's first federal fugitive slave law. Particularly tragic, both this law and its successor in 1850 stimulated an increase in the incidence of kidnapping and even provided the cloak of legal protection for kidnappers. Actually, the roots of the fugitive slave laws extend even further back, into the U.S. Constitution itself. While the term "slavery" does not appear in either the articles or the Bill of Rights, the practice of owning blacks was in fact sanctioned directly in five sections and indirectly in several others. One of the direct sanctions was the fugitive slave clause, found in Article 4, section 2. Slavery and the slave trade (Article 1, section 9) were tied by the framers of the Constitution more to the question of the authority of the state to control commerce than to any moral convictions among them on the subject of slavery. From the Constitution's very inception in 1787, southerners were thus using the states' rights defense to protect their interests, particularly slavery.[21]

The issues of both the slave trade and fugitive slaves engendered heated debates at the Constitutional Convention. Ironically, the first attack on slavery at the convention came from George Mason of Virginia, in criticism of the African slave trade. The demand of South Carolina Representatives Pierce Butler and Charles Pinckney for a fugitive slave clause also brought about protests from Pennsylvanian James Wilson and Roger Sherman of Connecticut. In both cases, though, northerners acquiesced, in return for the commerce clause, which gave Congress control over trade. This was the "dirty compromise," suggested by Pennsylvania representative Gouverneur Morris, that resulted in three sections in the Constitution.[22] The fugitive slave clause (Article 4, section 2) provided for delivery on demand of suspected fugitive slaves. Article 1, section 9, prevented Congress from interfering in the African slave trade until 1808 (although such transactions could be taxed, as explained in section 8). Section 8 of Article 1 gave Congress the power to regulate commerce.[23] Northern representatives could truthfully tell their constitutents that the word "slavery" had not even been

mentioned in the Constitution; southerners could assure
their constituents that slavery was protected in the document.[24] Or, as Staughton Lynd has described it, "If for
Northern delegates the motive was shame, for Southern
members of the convention it was prudence."[25] A precedent, therefore, had been established for the protection of
slavery even if it had not been stated explicitly in the Constitution.

The constitutional position on slavery would surface again
as the nation tried to find ways to grapple with the growing
issue. William Lloyd Garrison argued that the Constitution
was "a covenant of death," a pro-slavery document because it
gave southern states jurisdiction over slavery.[26] Political abolitionists like Salmon P. Chase claimed that the Founding Fathers' intention to limit slavery was implicit in their lack of
explicit federal support for slavery in the Constitution. Chase
argued that the 1793 Federal Fugitive Slave Law was a violation of the Constitution because Congress did not have the
power to legislate on the subject of slavery.[27]

Ironically, the nation's first federal fugitive slave law resulted not from an effort by the federal government to support slavery, but rather from one governor's attempt to help
a victim of kidnapping. The history of this law offers an ex-
cellent indication of the paradoxical nature of the legal system with regard to the problem of kidnapping specifically
and to free blacks generally. In May 1788, three Virginia men
kidnapped a free black, John Davis, from western Pennsylvania and sold him in Virginia. The Pennsylvania Abolition
Society asked for Governor Thomas Mifflin's help in returning Davis to freedom and in prosecuting his kidnappers. After Virginia Governor Beverley Randolph refused to comply
with Mifflin's request for assistance, Mifflin laid the matter
before President George Washington, who relayed the information to Congress. A committee in the House prepared a
bill designed to facilitate the extradition of fugitives from
justice; at the same time, they decided to prepare a law to
provide for the return of fugitives from labor.[28]

The result was the 1793 federal fugitive slave act. Two sections of the law dealt with the extradition of fugitives from justice, two with fugitive slaves. Although designed to effect the recovery of fugitives, the law actually gave kidnappers something approaching carte blanche to steal free blacks. As Wilbur H. Seibert, one of the early chroniclers of the Underground Railroad noted, "The method of proof prescribed by the measure was intended to facilitate the recovery of fugitives, but it was so slack that it encouraged the abduction of free negroes from the Northern states."[29] The law was obviously more concerned with protecting the right of slaveowners to recover their property than with the rights of persons claimed as slaves. The claimant needed only to take the suspected fugitive before any federal circuit or district court judge or magistrate in the state where the arrest was made. The requirement concerning proof of ownership was extremely vague; it could be established "either by oral testimony or affidavit taken before and certified by a magistrate of any such state or territory." The official then granted the claimant a certificate that enabled him or her to remove the suspect to the state from which the slave had allegedly fled.[30]

Because the person charged with being a slave was denied due process, the fugitive slave law facilitated kidnapping. Without due process, the victim's fate was in the hands of often unqualified, even unscrupulous magistrates. As witness Andrew Ellicott told the Congressional Committee on the African Slave Trade: "These poor, unprotected victims have been claimed as fugitive slaves, have been suddenly and secretly dragged before some magistrate selected for the special purpose, and such convenient magistrates have been found, who, on very loose and oral testimony, have with great facility furnished those cruel men with certificates, purporting to be in pursuance of the Act of Congress of February 12, 1793."[31]

Nearly twenty years later, Abner Forbes, teacher at a Boston school for blacks, told the Committee on the Domestic Slave Trade of the New England Anti-Slavery Society how the fugitive slave law continued to be utilized by kidnappers. Forbes reported that a Washington, D.C., man named Laskey, "a drunkard and spendthrift," had claimed a free black as a runaway advertised in a local paper. Forbes believed Laskey was paid by an accomplice, who took the victim south after a judge accepted Laskey's testimony and declared the suspect a slave. Forbes also said he thought that this kind of activity was so common that "any free colored man in *any* state may be, and a considerable number annually *is* kidnapped *according to law!*" (emphasis in original). The committee heard Forbes's testimony on the difficulty of getting white witnesses to testify to a black's freedom. Moreover, the financial burden on a black person accused of being a slave, although heavy, was according to Forbes irrelevant, for blacks were presumed to be slaves unless they could prove otherwise.[32]

Under the federal fugitive slave laws of 1793 and 1850, slaveowners could authorize agents to apprehend runaways and return them south. Legal slave catching became illegal kidnapping, however, when the person claimed as a fugitive slave was actually a free black. Sometimes this misjudgment was the result of a genuine mistake; sometimes it was deliberate. Antislavery author Jesse Torrey explained how kidnappers worked in pairs to misuse this law. A person pretending to be a slave catcher brought a free black into custody as a suspected fugitive slave. Then the accomplice appeared before a magistrate and claimed the suspect as his or her runaway slave. The kidnappers could then legally take their "slave" south to sell.[33]

George F. Alberti was probably the most infamous kidnapper to operate in this fashion. Nearly as well-known as the Cannon-Johnson family, Alberti worked in a much different manner, operating at the edge of the law rather than openly defying it. Alberti, a former Philadelphia constable, continued his career in law enforcement by working as a slave catcher in the city. Slaveowners hired him to recover their fugitive slaves, but he often went beyond the spirit of the law. Alberti was discovered trying to take free blacks into slavery so often that there could be no doubt of his intention to kidnap.

In 1851, George Alberti was tried and convicted under the Pennsylvania antikidnapping law of 1847.[34] He was found guilty of abducting baby Joel Henry Thompson from Philadelphia. The boy's mother, Betsey Galloway, also known as Catharine Thompson, apparently had run away from her owner, James Mitchell of Maryland. In 1845 she went to New Jersey with Will Thompson, a free black man, and gave birth to their son, Joel. In 1847 Mitchell authorized Alberti to return Galloway to slavery. Alberti arrested her in Philadelphia, where she admitted being Mitchell's slave. Alberti secured an alderman's certificate to take her to Maryland, and moved the woman, with her child, across the state line into Elkton.[35] Will Thompson got a warrant issued against Alberti for the kidnapping of his son Joel. Indicted by a grand jury, Alberti went to trial in February 1851. The prosecution argued that Joel was free because he had been born in New Jersey, a free state, and Alberti had no right to seize him.[36] Alberti claimed that he had not wanted to remove the child but had no other choice. "That woman of Mitchell's that I took insisted on taking her child with her," he argued. "I knew it was born in a free State, and I didn't want to let it go with her, but she begged to have it."[37]

Judge Parsons told the jury that Alberti did have a choice: he should have left both mother and child. The judge, who characterized the case as "without parallel in history,[38] fined George Alberti one thousand dollars and sentenced him to ten years in prison, while an accomplice received a slightly lesser sentence. This was not the end of the case, however. The incident became a cause célèbre and was an important issue in the 1851 Pennsylvania gubernatorial election. When he took office in 1852, Governor William Bigler, the Democrat who had campaigned against the state's personal liberty law, pardoned Alberti.[39]

The Pennsylvania Abolition Society was by that time well acquainted with Alberti's long career as legal slave catcher and illegal kidnapper. Possibly the earliest recorded evidence of Alberti's kidnapping activities was the case of Richard Keen, a free black seized in 1815 by Alberti and an accomplice, Joseph Robinson. The PAS initiated a suit against the two for abducting Keen and stealing his free papers. When the case finally came to trial in 1818, the two kidnappers were ordered to pay $250 in fines in addition to court costs.[40]

Such legal remedies did not deter Alberti from his chosen profession. The PAS was involved in numerous other cases in which Alberti had claimed free blacks as slaves. By 1839, the PAS was referring to Alberti as the "well known" kidnapper.[41] His reputation spread beyond the Philadelphia area to Baltimore; in 1837 the *Liberator* carried a report on Alberti's activities in that city. Two Baltimore policemen traveled to Philadelphia with a warrant from the governor of Maryland for Alberti's arrest. In Baltimore, Alberti and an accomplice, Andrew S. Smith, had been charged with obtaining money under false pretenses after kidnapping two Philadelphia blacks and selling them to Baltimore resident Hope S. Slater for eleven hundred dollars. When Slater discovered that the two were free, he swore out a complaint before the grand jury, which indicted Alberti and Smith.[42]

In 1850, Alberti was implicated in one of the first cases adjudicated under the second fugitive slave law, the celebrated Adam Gibson case. Alberti and two accomplices, William McKinley and Robert A. Smith, had seized Gibson in a philadelphia market and charged him with stealing chickens. Although they had no warrant, a gun to Gibson's head persuaded him to go with them to the office of Edward Ingraham, the city's federal fugitive slave commissioner. There Gibson was detained on charge of being an escaped slave from Cecil County, Maryland, named Emory Rice. While Gibson's attorneys were denied time to contact witnesses from New Jersey (where Gibson had been born) and Delaware who could attest to his freedom, Alberti produced a witness who identified Gibson as the slave Rice. The witness, J. Frisbee Price, at that point was under indictment for kidnapping, and his "hang-dog look," according to the *Pennsylvania Freeman*, "was quite in keeping with such a business."[43]

Gibson's counsel gave a persuasive argument, noting that

the descriptions of the two men did not match and that the only witness who claimed that Gibson was a slave was himself under indictment for kidnapping. Two other witnesses, black men who knew Gibson, attested to his free status. Nonetheless Commissioner Ingraham remanded Gibson to slavery and authorized Alberti to take him into Maryland. When the claimant, William S. Knight, saw Gibson, however, he told Alberti that he had brought back the wrong man. The slaveowner then provided for Gibson's return to Philadelphia. Alberti and several of his associates were arrested and stood trial for kidnapping Gibson.[44]

None of these brushes with the law, including his conviction for kidnapping in 1851, seem to have stopped George Alberti. He was certainly unrepentant in 1859 when a reporter for the *National Anti-Slavery Standard* interviewed Alberti at his home in Philadelphia. During the conversation, Alberti justified his actions with passages from the *Bible*. "No, sir, slavery is according to the law of God," he told the appalled abolitionist. "The slaveholder has as good a right to his niggers as he has to his horses; and if they run away, as a good citizen I have a right to catch them." Alberti also confirmed that his time in prison had not altered his opinion. "I would catch a nigger on Monday, if I had the chance." "On Monday?" the reporter queried. "Why not to-morrow?" "Because to-morrow is Sunday," Alberti replied. "I believe it would be a sin for me to do it on Sunday." Alberti closed the interview by responding to the reporter's question of how many blacks he had taken: "easy a hundred."[45]

Although the law certainly seemed to favor southerners in the recovery of fugitive slaves, as evidenced by the activities of agents like Alberti, slaveowners were not satisfied with the law and made numerous attempts to alter it.[46] Furthermore, northern resistance to the fugitive slave law sometimes made enforcement difficult. People refused to abide by the law, some going so far as to shelter suspected fugitives, while northern state legislatures passed personal liberty laws (see ch. 3) to negate the fugitive slave law's effectiveness. So southerners continued to press for a law to give them more control over the recovery process and allow them to bypass what they perceived to be northern interference. Not until 1850 did they succeed.

The Fugitive Slave Law of 1850 was much more specific and comprehensive than its predecessor, although not greatly different in content. The new law stated that testimony of the suspected fugitive was not permissible evidence: a suspect's protest that he or she was free need not be considered. Also, the right of habeas corpus did not apply to fugitives, so not even with help from white lawyers could a suspect be protected in this manner. In addition, the 1850 law increased the penalty for interference with the removal of a fugitive from five hundred to one thousand dollars.[47]

One of the most revealing aspects of the 1850 law was that it was administered by special commissioners appointed by U.S. circuit courts. They were paid ten dollars if they ordered the return of the suspect to slavery, five dollars if they released the suspect. Supposedly this difference in payments was justified by the amount of paperwork necessary, but some questioned this, countering that the arrangement served as a convenient financial inducement to slave catchers. For example, George M. Stroud, a Philadelphia judge who in 1856 compiled a book on laws relating to slavery, argued that the difference in fees had nothing to do with paperwork: if the commissioner decided to remand the victim to slavery, the certificate to be issued was the only extra work.[48]

Stroud showed that the form of most certificates required only about sixty words, and as the going rate for recorders was one cent for every ten words, the certificate cost a mere sixty cents to make. He asked, "Is it not demonstrable, therefore, that, in giving *five* dollars for these three minutes' labour, something more than *compensation* was intended to be offered?" The *Pennsylvania Freeman* was more direct, charging that "the provision . . . bribes the Commissioner to grant the claim of the slaveholder."[49]

As there was no appeals process, commissioners had the last word. With no check on this power, blacks, both free and slave, were completely at the mercy of the commissioners.[50]

Abolitionist John Gorham Palfrey noted, "The simple truth is, at this moment, that if an affidavit comes from Georgia that A.B. has escaped from service there, and somebody can be found to testify that I am A.B., and an unresponsible commissioner . . . chooses to say, for the fee of ten dollars, that he believes his testimony, I must go to Georgia . . . and there is no remedy for me whatever in the laws of my country."[51] Fellow abolitionist Wendell Phillips put it more succinctly: "The slave Commissioner sits omnipotent and his certificate is final."[52]

Some were decidedly uncomfortable with appointed officials' having so much power. George Stroud, for example, charged, "These commissioners were not originally selected upon any presumed judicial qualification. They were a species of inferior committing magistrates who sought the appointment for its perquisites."[53] Philadelphia Commissioner Edward D. Ingraham was described as "a man of strong feeling, prejudice, and determination, and decided in his views, not only as to the expediency, but as to the legality of slavery."[54] After Ingraham wrongly sent Adam Gibson into slavery in Maryland, a number of newspapers called for his resignation. The *Philadelphia Daily News* was perhaps the most harsh: "We have no idea of sustaining U.S. Commissioners who choose to convert themselves into willing kidnappers of free negroes."[55]

Numerous observers noted the parasitical connection between the fugitive slave law and kidnapping. Because suspects were denied due process, kidnappers used the law as a cover for their illegal activities,[57] just as they did in Kentucky. Kidnapping on both sides of the Ohio River increased after 1850.[58] The rate of kidnapping in Pennsylvania increased, as did its residents' dislike for the 1850 law.[59] David Potter summed up the law's significance for free blacks: "For years, this danger of being dragged away into slavery had made the life of the free Negro precarious, and it was undoubtedly accentuated by the new law."[60]

The two federal fugitive slave laws, while probably the best-known, were not the only laws that facilitated the illegal enslavement of free people of color. Numerous lesser-known state laws also produced the same result. For example, Southern states placed so many restrictions upon the process of freeing slaves that manumission laws became, in effect, antimanumission laws. The earliest such laws were passed in the eighteenth century, but most were made more restrictive beginning in the early 1800s.[61] Some states gave control of the emancipation process to the courts, as in Tennessee, or to the legislature, as in South Carolina. Alteration of manumission laws resulted in two developments that increased kidnapping. First, the door was opened for slaveowners to challenge legal manumissions, often those that had been effected in wills. Second, some states, such as Alabama and Florida, padded laws that required newly freed slaves to leave the state immediately or risk reenslavement.[62] By the 1850s, only a handful of southern states still allowed manumission at all.[63]

Benjamin Chelsom was one person victimized by such laws. A newspaper report described Chelsom as an escaped slave who worked on the Underground Railroad, helping fugitives from Kentucky across the Ohio River. Actually, Chelsom had been freed in his Kentucky owner's will of 1840, but the courts had set aside this portion of the will (after Chelsom had taken up residence in Ohio, a free state), and the heirs had been trying unsuccessfully to get Chelsom back ever since. Captured in the act of aiding fugitives, after a free black apparently hired by the heirs served as a decoy, Chelsom "fought with the desperation of a man who had once tasted the sweets of liberty." Several men managed to subdue him and deliver him to the Covington, Kentucky, jail, from which he was taken back into slavery.[64] The return to bondage of manumitted blacks continued throughout the mid-nineteenth century, and remained a matter of contention to the very eve of the Civil War. In 1858, the *Albany (New York) Evening Journal*, for example, discussed a recent court decision in Virginia arising out of the death of slaveowner John L. Poindexter. His will provided that upon his wife's death, his slaves were to be given the choice of becoming free persons or being sold. Manumission by will had been legal in

Virginia since 1782. But the heirs contested the will, and the Virginia Supreme Court of Appeals decided that the provision in the will giving slaves the choice of freedom was void, "the slaves having no legal capacity to make such election."[65]

Perhaps most disheartening about southern states' manumission laws were the amendments that required emancipated slaves to leave the state. Aside from the emotional toll this took on those forced to leave family and friends behind, the practical problems rendered freedom a near-impossibility in some cases. While most southern states had laws that forced newly manumitted slaves to leave, most also had laws forbidding free blacks to come into the state. Even assuming that most freed slaves wanted to settle in the North, how could they get there? Those not living in border states, or in seaports, had to travel through southern states where they were liable to be arrested, jailed, and then possibly sold into slavery. The story of Lunsford Lane was just one example of this dilemma.

Virginia prohibited black immigration in 1793, the first state to do so. By the 1830s, most southern states had followed suit, as had many western territories and even some northern states, such as Illinois.[66] In most cases these laws gave blacks enough time to leave the state before they faced prosecution. In Virginia, for example, the law took effect after a newly freed black remained in the state more than twelve months.[67] But the South Carolina grace period was only fifteen days, hardly sufficient time for someone traveling on foot to pass through the state, especially if he or she needed to stop and work for money along the way. Other states, such as Maryland and Mississippi, gave nonresident blacks a warning before their arrest.[68] Yet the danger free blacks faced once in custody was great. Laws were not always followed to the letter, and once free blacks found themselves jailed for any reason, many found it very difficult to leave except as slaves.

There is evidence that some Americans realized the inherent danger these laws posed for free blacks. The Committee on Judiciary Petitions, U.S. House of Representatives, received a series of appeals from citizens protesting anti-immigration laws in 1854. Residents of Ohio, Iowa, Kentucky, and Tennessee complained that these laws were unfair, because "free colored citizens . . . are liable to be . . . sold as slaves, without having committed any crime," a direct violation of the Constitution. Congress apparently did not respond to the petitions.[69]

State laws aimed at controlling black sailors who entered southern ports also played a role in kidnappings. Free black sailors, extremely vulnerable to seizure and sale as slaves, began carrying identification papers such as birth certificates and statements of citizenship to protect themselves against British impressment in the 1780s.[70] As additional insurance, in 1796 the federal government began issuing protection certificates to all American seamen.[71] For black sailors, these documents served a dual purpose—protection against seizure either by the British or by southern authorities. Because the papers specifically stated whether or not the bearer was "free," they could prevent a free black from being mistakenly incarcerated as a fugitive slave.[72] But laws passed by southern states in the antebellum period rendered this identification worthless.

Hoping to control and restrict their free black populations, southern states in the early nineteenth century made it illegal for black sailors to come ashore when ships docked in southern ports. Accordingly, black sailors were jailed from a ship's arrival until it sailed again, with the captain responsible for paying the jail fees. This put a heavy financial burden on the captains. In January 1850, for example, after the *Europa* sailed from Boston to Savannah, Captain Nathaniel Brown wrote to the ship's owners that police had jailed the black steward and cook "for safekeeping." He was obliged to hire replacements and to pay the fees of the jailed men; the total bill came to more than $150.[73] Unscrupulous captains often found it easier to sail without their black hands to avoid paying both their jail costs and remaining wages.

One sailor with firsthand knowledge of this practice was New Yorker Stephen Dickinson, a fireman on the *New Cas-*

tle in 1837. Upon arrival in New Orleans, he and "the other colored boys" were ordered by the mate to go with him to get some hemp. Instead they were put in jail, where they were whipped for saying that they were free. Transferred to Vicksburg, the men were sold by a slave trader named Botts, who apparently had made a deal with the ship's captain. Dickinson was enslaved in Kentucky, where, after several years, he found a white man willing to help him regain his freedom: a neighboring farmer, Thomas Vantreese, who took Dickinson's case to a lawyer. When the sheriff informed Dickinson's master, the slaveowner fled with Dickinson to New Orleans. There Dickinson found another lawyer, a former New York resident, who took his case. The result was that Dickinson was freed and his owner, James Percival, recovered $600 of the $950 he had paid the trader Botts. Percival then claimed that the former slave owed him $200 and took charge of Dickinson's free papers until the debt was paid. After working on several ships to earn the money, Dickinson was advised by his lawyer simply to leave the South, and the former seaman returned to New York after an absence of nearly three years.[74]

Dickinson's experience under the Negro seamen acts was not unique; many black sailors faced similar dangers. In the early nineteenth century, about 20 percent of Philadelphia's two thousand sailors were black.[75] Blacks represented 20 percent of the seamen in Providence, Rhode Island, at a time when they were only 4 percent of the city's population.[76] But the issue concerned not only black seamen but also the governments of northern states and other nations attempting to protect the rights of their citizens. In fact, the debate over the Negro seamen acts escalated into a diplomatic battle between the United States and Great Britain.

South Carolina enacted the first Negro seamen act in 1822, in response to the Denmark Vesey rebellion in Charleston.[77] Henry Elkison, a British sailor jailed under the statute, sued and won a favorable decision. Judge William Johnson of the U.S. circuit court in Charleston, a native Charlestonian and member of U.S. Supreme Court, declared the act unconstitutional in 1823, but his decision was disregarded by South Carolina, and the jailing of black sailors continued.[78] Ironically, in light of earlier British impressment of American citizens, Britain began in 1822 to issue formal complaints to the United States on this subject.[79] The practice of kidnapping blacks from British ships, continued, however. As late as 1859 the British Board of Trade issued warnings to ship captains to make certain their black sailors had proof of identity when traveling to America.[80]

One British seaman who was victimized by this law was John Glasgow, resident of Liverpool. Born in British Guiana, he went to sea as a cabin boy early in life. In 1830, at about age twenty-five, he worked on an English ship bound for Savannah, Georgia, to take on a cargo of rice. There he was detained under a Georgia law that ordered the incarceration of free blacks entering the state. Such laws continued to be applied in Georgia and in other states despite the Elkison decision.[81] With mounting delays in his ship's departure, Glasgow's jail bill escalated, as did the cost of paying a substitute to do his work while he was incarcerated. When the captain refused to pay for his release, Glasgow was sold as a slave to Thomas Stevens of Baldwin County for $350. There Glasgow worked on a plantation, where he was whipped for declaring he was free and British. Glasgow's story was related by a fellow slave who escaped from the plantation; he did not know what became of John Glasgow.[82]

Though northern officials such as John Quincy Adams expressed sympathy, the federal government refused to take action against the southern states.[83] Boston, the home of many black sailors, protested in Congress. Massachusetts Representative Robert C. Winthrop asked the House to take up the following resolutions: 1) that the imprisonment of black sailors on no charge was a violation of their rights of citizenship, as stated in Article 4, section 2, of the Constitution; 2) that the same applied to foreign sailors as well (Article 6); and 3) that states using these laws interfered with Congress's authority to regulate commerce. Winthrop's propositions were laid on the table without debate, however, and the House took no action against the southern laws.[84]

When it became apparent that the federal government would not intervene, both Britain and the state of Massachusetts took more direct action by seeking a settlement with the southern states. Massachusetts sent former Congressman Samuel Hoar to Charleston in 1844 to negotiate a compromise on the laws, but he met with only threats of violence. When he arrived in Charleston, Hoar sent a letter to South Carolina Governor James H. Hammond, which was received with marked hostility when it was read in the state legislature. The local police warned Hoar that his life was in danger, but the Massachusetts envoy replied that he had a job to do; he had come armed with a list of Boston sailors jailed in the city whose freedom he intended to negotiate. The threats escalated, and within a short time Hoar was forced to concede defeat: "It seemed to me then that there was but one question for me to settle, which was whether I should walk to a carriage or be dragged to it." Henry Hubbard, a lawyer who was appointed Massachusetts agent in Louisiana, met with a similar fate in that state.[85]

The British fared only slightly better. In the decade before the Civil War, although British representatives failed to negotiate the repeal of the Negro seamen acts, they were successful in reducing the restrictions placed upon their black sailors.[87] The Negro seamen acts resurfaced in Congress in 1850 during discussion about the abolition of the slave trade in the District of Columbia. Robert C. Winthrop of Massachusetts set off a heated debate in the Senate when he read a letter he had received from a Boston ship's captain, Charles A. Ranlett, who traded frequently in New Orleans. In the letter, Ranlett claimed that hundreds of free black sailors had been jailed in various southern ports under the laws. He recounted an incident in which black members of his own crew were imprisoned in Charleston. When he went to reclaim them, he saw many others likewise jailed. Ranlett concluded, "A list nearly as long as the longest abolition petition could be made out of names of free colored men who have been taken out of ships in Charleston, Mobile, and New Orleans for only being black." Ranlett's letter was immediately challenged by several senators from southern states. Arthur Butler of South Carolina and Mississippian Jefferson Davis insisted that the laws were necessary to protect southern whites and their property against infiltration of northern free black agents bent on fomenting slave insurrection. Further, the senators added, the laws were not nearly as draconian as Winthrop and his sources made them out to be. Butler claimed that no one had ever actually been sold under the laws. (We can only wonder whether he truly believed this.) Senators Pierre Soule and Solomon Downs of Louisiana and John Berrien of Georgia claimed that free black sailors were not even imprisoned in their states, although laws authorizing incarceration were on the books. Even if free black sailors were sold as slaves, Butler asserted, the fault lay with the captains who had abandoned them rather than with southern laws.[87]

In an effort to clear Ranlett's name and add support to his contentions, Winthrop later asked for a series of documents to be added to the record. In addition to jail bills, several letters from ships' captains attesting to the function of the Negro seamen acts demonstrated that the southern senators were mistaken. It appeared that Winthrop purposely included statements from captains whose sailors had been imprisoned in New Orleans and Savannah, a direct contradiction of the claims of the Louisiana and Georgia senators that the laws were not enforced in their states. The testimony of John H. Pearson, ship owner of Boston, was particularly revealing. Pearson first established his credibility by explaining that he had, at great expense to himself, effected the return of two fugitive slaves who had stowed away on one of his ships. In a shocking statement regarding the Negro seamen acts, he informed Winthrop, "If it should be found necessary to sustain you in your remarks, certificates could be forwarded of more than one thousand imprisonments, within three years, at the port of New Orleans alone."[88] No wonder black sailors were deeply concerned about the risk that they ran in working in "the nation's single most important antebellum domestic trade—freighting southern cotton to northern ports." Lack of viable alternatives, however, forced many to take the risk.[89]

In addition to sailors entering southern ports, free blacks of other categories could be sold into slavery for a variety of reasons. In Maryland and Virginia, free blacks could be enslaved for crimes that carried terms of imprisonment. North Carolina made it legal to sell free blacks who were unable to pay their taxes. In Mississippi, any black person who could not prove free status could be sold into slavery. And in Florida, blacks who were deemed "idle and dissolute" were liable to enslavement.[90]

Of the free blacks legally sold into slavery, however, most had been jailed as suspected fugitives. Ironically, the lack of a claimant failed to prove a suspect's free status. Rather, it allowed the victim to be sold. Various southern states had laws like Tennessee's, which authorized the sale of unclaimed runaways after twelve months.[91] Southern newspapers were replete with advertisements offering for sale black people who claimed to be free. In 1825, for example, the *National Intelligencer* of Washington, D.C., gave notice of the sale of three young black men who said that they were free but who had been jailed as suspected fugitives. If unclaimed, they would be "sold for their jail fees, and other expenses, as the law directs."[92] The *Woodville Republican*, a Mississippi paper, sought the owner of alleged runaway Henry Williams, who claimed to be free. If not repossessed, "he will be dealth with as the law directs."[93] Others were more circumspect. Beginning in June 1835, the *Vicksburg Register* ran an advertisement for the owner of a twenty-seven-year-old "boy" known only as Bob. Bob, who stated that he was free, was advertised as a fugitive slave. After the notice ran for six months but no one appeared as Bob's owner, Warren County Sheriff E. W. Morris announced his intention to sell Bob to the highest bidder outside the courthouse on January 18, 1836.[94]

Certainly, some of the persons jailed as fugitives who claimed free status were in fact slaves. The *Woodville Republican* of December 22, 1838, carried an ad seeking "Dave," a runaway slave from Louisiana. The notice was placed by his master, who reported that Dave "has sometimes endeavored to pass himself off as free."[95] Regardless of how many suspected fugitives were in fact free and how many were in fact slaves claiming to be free, the law presumed all blacks to be slaves unless they could prove otherwise. Even if they could produce free papers, authorities might reject that proof as a forgery. Even when no owner appeared, the suspected fugitive could be sold to cover jail fees. The burden lay solely on black shoulders, those least equipped to bear it.

A final type of legal enslavement of free people occurred when a master refused to honor the free status of a slave who had purchased his or her freedom or who had been manumitted. Often slaveowners or their heirs refused to abide by agreements that had been made to free their slaves. In this way, too, indentured servants could be held as virtual slaves beyond the time stipulated for their term of service.

One of the earliest such cases was that of Moses, a manumitted slave of North Carolina. A certificate of emancipation dated November 4, 1776, shows that Caleb Trueblood, resident of Pasquotank County, had freed his slave Moses. Yet a newspaper advertisement dated October 19, 1785, offered a reward for the same Moses then accused of being a runaway.[96]

The agreement between Anthony Williams and his master, Matthias Hite of Virginia, is another example of a slaveowner's refusing to honor a legal emancipation agreement. In July of 1792, the two entered into a contract. If Williams served Hite for eight years, he would be given his freedom, as well as a horse and bridle worth ten pounds. After eight years, Hite wrote Williams the following letter:

> To Tone   July 1800
> Tone This is the day I ment to set you Free from Slavery and as you broke and violated your part of the agree-

ment I will yet do this if you will stay peaceably until
my harvest is secured in the stalks I will then step into
Court and Emansupate from all men according to law if
you will not consent to this I shall not free you as no
law can compell me to.

[Signed] M. Hite

Hite was mistaken. Williams sued for his freedom, and a
jury declared him a free man and awarded him damages of
$11.50. This case was atypical, however. Williams was the
only Monongalia County slave to sue successfully for freedom.[97]

Some Americans, of course, were outraged by this constant disregard for human rights. Not surprisingly, the *Liberator* was at the forefront of such protests. In 1838, it carried
an excerpt from a Kentucky newspaper stating that a free
black citizen of Boston, John Barnwell, had been jailed in
Henderson County, Kentucky. The jailer charged that he had
corresponded with a resident of Boston and had come to the
conclusion that Barnwell had never lived there. Included
with the *Liberator's* account was a statement of outrage from
another abolitionist newspaper, the *Emancipator*, which questioned the credibility of the Boston resident: "Still less do we
know that he is authorized privately to certify away the liberties of a native of Boston?"[98]

William Allen, a black abolitionist, addressed a similar concern in a speech he delivered in Leeds, England. He informed
his audience that any black person found in the American capital was liable to be sold into slavery, and he suggested that
greed was the basic motive. After jail fees were paid, any extra
money from the sale of a prisoner went to the jailer. One well-
known jailer whose name appeared frequently in *National Intelligencer* advertisements for the sale of free blacks, Tench
Ringold, had, according to Allen, "made a fortune by this
traffic."[99]

Abolitionists in Congress also attempted to raise public
awareness of the problems for free blacks caused by the various sorts of antiblack laws. In December 1843, in the House,
Ohio Representative Joshua Giddings presented a petition

from William Jones, a free black incarcerated for no reason in Washington, D.C., and about to be sold for jail fees. Jones sought help from Congress, but the House voted against considering his request.[100]

Others went beyond complaining and worked for the repeal of state laws that permitted the sale of free blacks. In 1828, Representative Charles Miner of Pennsylvania urged Congress to abolish slavery in the District of Columbia, one of his reasons being the prevention of kidnapping. Miner's personal investigation had resulted in the discovery of nearly three hundred alleged fugitives in District jails, many of them free, who had been sold as slaves. Miner reminded his colleagues that the issue of kidnapping and enslavement for inability to pay jail fees had been discussed by Congress as early as 1816. He succeeded in getting the committee on the District of Columbia to consider his charges, but no action was taken. Indeed, more than twenty years elapsed before Congress abolished the slave trade in the District of Columbia as part of the Compromise of 1850.[101]

The legislature of Maine sent a similar request to Congress in 1844, requesting the repeal of state and territorial laws "which render persons of color liable to arrest and imprisonment and to be sold for jail fees." Such laws, the petition argued, were unconstitutional, and it urged members of Congress to work within their states to repeal them. The request was sent to the Senate Committee on the District of Columbia, but in June the Senate voted to discharge the committee from further consideration of the resolution.[102]

Once again, public officials refused to help eradicate kidnapping by altering the many laws that facilitated it. Of course the law did not always work to the disadvantage of free blacks, as kidnapping was a crime in the majority of states, even in the South. While enforcement was sporadic at best, these laws did give fair-minded governors and mayors the opportunity to protect their free black populations.

CHAPTER THREE

"Leave No Stone Unturned": Government Assistance to Free Blacks

The kidnapping of free blacks for sale as slaves was prohibited in most states, including those in the South. State antikidnapping laws offered some measure of protection to free people of color, as did northern personal liberty laws, passed in response to the federal fugitive slave laws.

But this is not to suggest that the legal system and the government worked to the advantage of free blacks. Kidnapping flourished despite its illegality. Protective laws needed enforcement in order to be effective, and they were upheld only sporadically at best. It was also difficult to prosecute the majority of kidnapping cases because they involved interstate travel. Since no federal antikidnapping law was passed before the Civil War, the battle against kidnapping depended on cooperation between the states. Abolitionists constantly petitioned their state governments for stronger penalties against kidnapping and better enforcement of antikidnapping laws. As the *Liberator* clearly stated, "The liberty of colored free men has not been sufficiently guarded by the laws of the United States, nor any of the separate states."[1] But several government officials stand out as strong supporters of antikidnapping legislation. Joseph Watson, the Philadelphia mayor who worked tirelessly to free the victims of the Cannon-Johnson gang, was certainly a champion of the law. Governors, particularly in Ohio, New York, and Pennsylvania, worked at the state level to assist kidnapped free blacks.

Vermont enacted the first state antikidnapping law in 1787, and all northern states except Rhode Island followed with similar legislation. The majority of northwestern territories followed suit as they gained statehood. Five slave states (Delaware, Virginia, Tennessee, Georgia, Mississippi), as well as the District of Columbia, also had antikidnapping laws. Most of these statutes carried heavy penalties for infractions, such as Pennsylvania's law of 1826, which levied up to two thousand dollars in fines and twenty-one years in prison.[2]

Even in those states that did not ultimately enact antikidnapping laws, considerable sentiment for such laws existed. In 1790, 1817, and 1818, Maryland Quakers, for example, petitioned their state legislature for an antikidnapping law. In 1816, a grand jury in Baltimore had heard evidence on this topic. Its intent was to investigate the slave trade, but it quickly determined that "slaves lawfully held are not the only victims of this barbarity." The grand jury report stated that indentured servants were very vulnerable to kidnapping, as were free blacks, and added that slaves were stolen as well. It concluded that "the horrible practice of kidnapping both the slaves and the free instead of being checked by the vigilance and exertion of our police is increasing with enormous rapidity." The solution, jurors felt, was an antikidnapping law.[3] However, the Maryland legislature apparently did not enact such legislation.

Those states that had antikidnapping legislation often debated strengthening these laws, as in Delaware. An antikidnapping law had been in effect since 1787, but many there believed that it was not stringent enough. In 1817, numerous petitions were sent to Dover complaining that the kidnapping of free blacks from the state had become a grave problem, and stronger laws were needed to prevent the practice.[4] The legislature took no action at the time, however, and twenty years later state officials were still grappling with the problem. In a message to the Delaware legislature in 1839, Governor Cornelius P. Comegys noted the connection between enslavement of free blacks and the state's practice of leasing its convicts for work outside the state. He wanted to abolish the hiring out of white prisoners altogether and to permit the hiring out of black convicts only within the state.

This practice was brutal for white prisoners, the governor argued, but even worse for black convicts. Although the leasing of a black prisoner as a servant was limited to a specific number of years, in reality "perpetual slavery in the South is his inevitable doom." Once black convicts left the borders of Delaware, "all chance of restored freedom is gone." In fact, Comegys believed that none of the black prisoners hired for work outside the state had ever returned.[5]

It was also from Delaware that the first call for a federal antikidnapping law emanated. On behalf of his absent colleague from Delaware, U.S. Representative Albert Gallatin of Pennsylvania presented a resolution from the Delaware legislature in April 1796 requesting that Congress take action against kidnapping. The Delaware legislators argued that beyond their state's measures against the practice, Congress must exercise its jurisdiction over trade across state lines and waterways if kidnapping was to be stopped.[6]

The Committee on Commerce and Manufacturing, agreeing with the Delaware legislature that the problem of kidnapping went beyond state control, proposed as a solution that ships' captains be required to carry a listing of all blacks on board and their status. Ironically, the debate on the floor suggested that the main objection to any federal action was the fear that somehow slaves would be freed as a result of antikidnapping legislation. The House voted to postpone consideration until more information could be gathered. A month later, the committee declared in its report that it was "not expedient for this House to interfere with any existing law of the states on this subject." Thus, the first debate on antikidnapping in Congress ended without any action being taken.[7]

Congress discussed a federal antikidnapping law again in 1816. In March, John Randolph called upon the House "to put a stop to proceedings at that moment carried on under their very noses; proceedings that were a crying sin before God and man; a practice which . . . was not surpassed for abomination in any part of the earth." The Virginia congressman referred to slavery in the District of Columbia, particularly to those blacks incarcerated and sold there who were actually kidnapped free people. House members decided to appoint a special committee, chaired by Randolph, to investigate the issue. This was ironic as Randolph, a southerner and a slaveholder, had voted against a bill to end the African slave trade. Randolph declared that as a result he had been "falsely held up, as one of the advocates of the most nefarious, the most disgraceful, and the most infernal traffic that has ever stained the annals of the human race." Randolph had not supported the bill, he claimed, only because it would interfere with the right of Americans to own slaves.[8]

The committee took depositions and received letters on the subject of slavery in the nation's capital. Much of this correspondence discussed kidnapping. Francis Scott Key, a lawyer and professor at Georgetown College, Jesse Torrey, abolitionist and author, and Chief Justice William Cranch of the District of Columbia Circuit Court, were among those who shared knowledge of kidnapped free blacks jailed and/ or sold in the District. Key referred to "the frequent seizure of free persons who are hurried off in the night brought to the City and transported as slaves," and added, "I have no doubt . . . that many are carried away as slaves who are entitled to freedom."[9] If the committee presented a report, it went unrecorded; nor was any action taken by Congress.

The following year, another congressional committee, this one on the African slave trade, also heard evidence of kidnapping. One witness, Andrew Ellicott of Baltimore, reinforced the claim of the Delaware legislature that because so many kidnapping victims were taken across state lines, state officials could not prosecute. "The Cases are extremely numerous in which free persons are carried off by Water and by Land," Ellicott stated. "In fact they are continually occurring." Residents of Pennsylvania and Delaware also provided the committee with information concerning kidnapping, as did Baltimore mayor Elisha Tyson. Tyson explained that he had rescued many victims of kidnapping and added, "I have reason to believe the number who are clandestinely carried off beyond the reach of discovery is immensely greater."[10]

Pressure on Washington to enact federal antikidnapping legislation continued, especially from the Quakers and other abolitionists. Nearly twenty years after he had testified in Washington, Jesse Torrey, who had published two books on slavery during the interim, gave evidence on kidnapping at an abolitionist convention. In 1834, the New England Anti-Slavery Society appointed a committee to investigate the internal slave trade. Its report revealed the extent of kidnapping, as described by Torrey, newspaper editor Hezekiah Niles, and Philadelphia judge George M. Stroud, among others. The committee recommended that a petition be sent to inform Congress of these activities.[11] Although Congress sometimes debated such petitions there is no evidence that a federal antikidnapping law was considered before the Civil War. Congress finally enacted antikidnapping legislation in 1866, after the abolition of slavery. This law made it illegal "to kidnap or carry away any other person, whether negro, mulatto or otherwise, with the intent that such other person shall be sold or carried into involuntary servitude or held as a slave."[12]

It was on the state level that black needs for protection against kidnapping were first recognized by law. Beyond simply listing antikidnapping laws on their books, several states enacted personal liberty laws to offer greater protection to those claimed under the federal fugitive slave law. State officials showed that state antikidnapping provisions could be effective when carried out by concerned parties.

Although commonly associated with the 1850 federal fugitive slave law, most states' personal liberty laws were a reaction to the 1793 U.S. law. The majority were passed in response to an 1842 court case, *Prigg v. Pennsylvania*. This case concerned the status of Margaret Morgan, who, although legally a slave, had been allowed to live as free all of her life. In 1832, she married a free black man, Jerry Morgan, and they moved from Maryland to Pennsylvania. Five years later, her owner's heiress hired Edward Prigg, a professional slave catcher, to return Morgan and her children to Maryland.[13]

A Pennsylvania act of 1826 required slaveowners and their

agents to obtain a certificate from a state official before removing a suspected fugitive from the state. This act was a revision of an 1820 law that had prohibited certain state officials from enforcing the 1793 fugitive slave law. The revised statute represented an attempt to provide a greater balance between the rights of slaveowners and those of accused fugitives. The state, then, tried to place itself between the federal government and individuals by requiring slaveowners to obtain a warrant from state authorities.[14] Without seeking a warrant, Prigg took Morgan and her children (at least one of whom had been born in Pennsylvania and was therefore free) to Maryland. He was then indicted for kidnapping under the Pennsylvania law and found guilty by the Pennsylvania Supreme Court.[15]

The U.S. Supreme Court reversed this decision, however, declaring the Pennsylvania statute unconstitutional because the power to legislate on the return of fugitives belonged to the federal government. Therefore, the requirement that a slavecatcher obtain a certificate from state authorities was not legal. Even more of a blow to free blacks, however, was the court's interpretation of the 1793 federal fugitive slave law. In the majority opinion, Justice Joseph Story declared that slaveowners had a "right of self-help" to obtain their property without interference. As long as they did not disturb the peace, slaveowners could remove their slaves without any judicial procedure.[16]

While the response to the Prigg decision among abolitionists was heated, the general public accepted the decision.[17] Despite the "open invitation for the kidnapping of free blacks," some historians have viewed the Prigg case as a victory, albeit a mixed one, for abolitionists.[18] This view refers to the third and perhaps best-known part of the Prigg decision. Though Justice Story wrote that states could not interfere with the enforcement of federal laws, he noted that they were not obliged to carry them out. It was this statement that provided the legal opening for the passage of personal liberty laws.[19]

Although most northerners did not directly obstruct enforcement of the federal law, abolitionists used the Prigg decision to make fugitive recapture much more cumbersome. When state officials refused to help, claimants had to turn to federal authorities, sometimes a great burden in terms of distance and time spent in seeking out federal officials.[20]

In 1843, for example, both Massachusetts and Vermont passed laws that made it illegal for state judges and justices of the peace to enforce the 1793 act. Some states, such as Ohio, also prohibited the use of state jails for holding suspected fugitives and imposed heavy penalties for disobeying these laws. In Vermont, any official or private citizen who aided in the seizure of a suspected fugitive faced a fine of as much as one thousand dollars and a five-year prison term.[21]

Some personal liberty laws actually functioned as antikidnapping laws to protect the rights of free black citizens of the North against illegal seizure under the Fugitive Slave Act of 1850. Four states—Massachusetts, Vermont, Michigan, and Wisconsin—extended the right of habeas corpus to suspected fugitive slaves, thereby giving blacks the right to protection against illegal imprisonment. The same four states also gave suspected runaways the right to a jury trial. These laws reflected an attempt to restore constitutional rights that had been removed by the 1850 law.[22]

But laws designed to protect a state's free black population were effective only when put into action by concerned public officials. New York officials distinguished themselves in the battle against kidnapping. In 1826, for example, Governor DeWitt Clinton came to the rescue of Gilbert Horton, a free black man jailed as a fugitive in Washington, D.C. Horton's case first came to light in August 1826, when John Owen, a paper mill owner living near Bedford, New York, received a package wrapped in a recent edition of the Washington *National Intelligencer*. The newspaper contained a notice for the owner of the "runaway" Gilbert Horton to claim him. Owen took the notice to his neighbor, Judge William Jay. They wrote to the District of Columbia marshal, offering proof of Horton's free status, and organized a meeting of citizens from Westchester County to discuss the incident. With Jay acting as secretary, the group decided to ask the governor to demand Horton's release.[23]

Governor Clinton passed the resolutions on to President John Quincy Adams and asked that Horton be freed. The New York governor argued that any law that allowed a free person, a citizen of the United States, to be jailed and then sold as a slave was unconstitutional. Since the District of Columbia, where Horton was incarcerated, was under exclusive control of the federal government, Clinton asked the President to effect the victim's release. Adams sent the Westchester resolutions along with a letter he himself wrote to Secretary of State Henry Clay, who secured Horton's release.[24]

William Jay, son of Supreme Court Justice John Jay, recognized that although justice had prevailed in Horton's case, free people would continue to be enslaved as long as laws allowing for the seizure and sale of free blacks existed. Jay was convinced that one important way to prevent such incidents was to outlaw the slave trade in the District of Columbia. As requested by the Westchester resolutions, he drafted a memorial to Congress. Aaron Ward, representative for Westchester County, introduced the memorial, but there is no record that any legislative action followed.[25]

A decade and a half later, another New York governor distinguished himself in the fight against kidnapping. In 1840, William S. Seward signed into law the guarantee of the right to a jury trial for suspected fugitive slaves. Under the law, suspects were released if the claimants could not prove ownership. If claimants continued to attempt to secure the person, they faced a possible ten years in prison. Another law passed that year gave the governor the power to hire agents to return kidnapping victims. The following year, Seward also signed the repeal of the "nine months" law, which freed slaves nine months after they were brought into the state. With the repeal of the law, they became free immediately.[26]

Seward also intervened in several cases of New York blacks who were about to be illegally enslaved. In 1840, he helped secure the release of James Seward of Mexico, New York, who had been held as a fugitive in a New Orleans jail.

Two years later, the governor provided assistance to another victim, John Lewis, a cook who had been imprisoned as directed by Louisiana law when his ship docked in New Orleans.[27]

Efforts to restore the freedom of kidnapped free blacks continued in New York during the Civil War. Free black George Armstrong departed Watertown, New York, in the spring of 1860 with a man named Benjamin. Nothing was heard from Armstrong until his sister received a letter from a Washington, D.C., law firm, which stated that her brother had been jailed there as a runaway slave. After the facts of the case were brought before the governor, the state spent $242 to secure Armstrong's freedom—the cost of hiring an attorney, sending an agent and witnesses to Washington, buying Armstrong new clothes, and transporting him back home.[28]

Subsequently, governors in other states followed the precedent set in New York. In the late 1850s, Ohio's first Republican governor, Salmon P. Chase, and his successor, William Dennison, refused to extradite a free black man wanted for helping a fugitive slave escape from Kentucky. In a curious twist on southern appeals to states' rights, these northern governors argued the primacy of their authority to contravene federal law in defense of black civil rights. In 1861, Dennison's case went to the U.S. Supreme Court, which rendered a unanimous decision in favor of the Ohio governors (interestingly, the opinion was written by Chief Justice Roger B. Taney, best known for his opinion in the antiblack Dred Scott decision).[29]

Others governors who attempted to address the problem of kidnapping were sometimes thwarted by their own legislatures. In his inaugural address of 1822, Illinois Governor Edward Coles, a Virginia native who had moved to Illinois in 1819 in order to free his own slaves, requested that the legislature repeal the state's "black laws" and establish an antikidnapping law. He declared kidnapping "a crime which . . . was too often committed with impunity in the State," and committees were formed in both chambers of the legislature to consider a new law. The Senate reported that there was no way to pass such a law without altering the state constitution. The House produced a bill against kidnapping but it was tabled.[30]

The Peyton Polly case clearly illustrates the commitment of some public officials to upholding the rights of free blacks. Prosecution of the Peyton Polly kidnapping case lingered in the courts for a decade and cost the state of Ohio more than three thousand dollars, yet both the legislature and several governors persevered in the battle to restore the victims to freedom.

In January 1849, Douglas Polly, an emancipated slave, purchased his brother Peyton's seven children from David and Nancy Campbell, slaveowners of Pike County, Kentucky, at a cost of about eight hundred dollars. Douglas Polly then freed the children by moving them to Lawrence County, the southernmost county in Ohio, a free state. After living there for nearly a year, they were forcibly abducted on the night of June 6, 1850, by a gang who returned them to Kentucky.[31]

According to depositions taken in Catlettsburg, Kentucky, in May 1851, the Polly children's story was well known. Apparently the Campbells had told many area residents of their sale of the Pollys and their uncle's intention to set them free in Ohio. This was, in the words of deponent John Rowe, "common talk in the nighborhood for months before they left." The kidnappers then had no difficulty in finding the Pollys. James Sperry, one of the gang, told another deponent, John G. Medington, that Sperry and several others had gone to the Pollys' new home in Ohio and had broken open the door with an ax. They drove "the old man" (Peyton Polly, Sr.) out of the house and onto the roof by shooting at him, "grazing the wool on the top of his head." They then took the children back across the Ohio River into Kentucky.[32]

Details remain unclear, but apparently the kidnappers had been hired by an ironically named resident of Pikeville, Kentucky, David Justice, who paid them several hundred dollars each. Justice had apparently contemplated taking the Polly children in September 1849, soon after they moved to Ohio. His brother-in-law, attorney Jacob Heaberling, stated that Justice had offered him a thousand dollars for assisting in their return to Kentucky. Justice showed Heaberling a bill of sale for the Pollys, but when pressed by the attorney, admitted it was false. Heaberling's testimony was supported by that of farmer Colman Walker (who employed one of the Pollys), who also recalled Justice's "legal" attempt to claim the Pollys that fall. Thwarted in his efforts to obtain the family in this manner, Justice had then had them abducted.[33]

After the kidnapping, Justice claimed the Pollys as his property. He then sold four of the Polly children in Kentucky and four to slaveowner William Ratcliffe of Virginia. Early in 1851, the Ohio Assembly passed a resolution authorizing funds for the governor to inquire into and prosecute the matter. Governor Reuben Wood immediately appointed attorney Joel W. Wilson as the state's agent to investigate.[34]

The outcome of the Pollys' case showed the caprice of state jurisdiction in kidnapping cases. The four Pollys sold in Kentucky met a somewhat different fate from those enslaved in Virginia. In their former home state, the Polly children sued Jerome Watson and Alfred O. Robards for holding them illegally in slavery. They were declared free by the Louisville chancery court in October 1851.[35] The circuit court at Lexington as well as the Kentucky Court of Appeals upheld this decision.[36] Ohio attorney Ralph Leete informed Wood's successor, Governor William Medill, of the final resolution of the case and asked that Kentucky Attorney General James Harlan and his associates be paid for their hard work, as provided by the Ohio Assembly's resolution. He added that the four Pollys would need an escort from Kentucky to Ohio.[37] They arrived in Ohio two days later.[38]

The members of the Polly family sold in Virginia did not fare so well. Work on the Virginia case began as early as on the Kentucky case.[39] The case was scheduled to begin on October 11, 1851, but was postponed.[40] Not until August of the following year did the lawyers make another report. Joel Wilson then wrote to Governor Wood to explain that he had been to Barboursville, Virginia, to examine the depositions taken in the case. The kidnappers, he said, were collecting additional evidence and had been granted another continuance to obtain the testimony of important witnesses in Kentucky. Wilson sardonically reported, "It cannot be denied that they are strengthening their defense by testimony, but mostly of such persons as were either directly involved in the kidnapping, or their relatives or dependents."[41]

Fear of reprisal beset the prosecution. George Summers, an attorney from Kanawha County who was working for Ralph Leete recording depositions in Cabell County during the fall of 1851, asked to be excused from further involvement in the case because he had been frightened by the threats of kidnapper David Justice.[42] This intimidation continued throughout the next year, for as Joel Wilson reported, "The kidnappers promise to take my head off if I come again into their neighborhood." Unlike Summers, however, Wilson stated that it would take more than threats to stop him from working on the case.[43]

In 1853, three years after the kidnapping, the case of *Peyton Polly* v. *William Ratcliffe* finally went to trial in Cabell County, Virginia. Ratcliffe had apparently purchased the four Pollys from David Justice or his agents. Although they had been enslaved in Wayne County, the Pollys were brought on a writ of habeas corpus before Judge Samuel McComas in Cabell County. In the trial there, the Pollys were declared free, but on appeal the higher court decided that the case should have been heard in Wayne County, where the defendant resided. At this point, the case truly languished.[44]

Ohio lawyer Ralph Leete expressed his frustration with the legal system. The Virginia case had to be tried again, he wrote the new Ohio governor, Salmon P. Chase, and testimony retaken, with all the difficulty of finding the witnesses at a great cost to the state. The lawsuit had now been in progress for five years, while the Pollys remained in slavery. "Yet it is wrong to let the case be abandoned now; if the Federal Government could spend $100,000 to reduce *one* man to slavery, certainly the State of Ohio should not withhold the necessary amount of means to restore *three* persons to freedom." (One of the Pollys at issue had died since the suit was first brought.)[45]

Chase apparently shared Leete's concerns, for in an earlier letter to another lawyer in the case, John Laidley, Chase had explained that prosecution of the Kentucky part of the case had already cost the state of Ohio a large amount of money and the legislature was reluctant to continue supplying funds. Chase, however, wanted Laidley to continue; he asked only that the lawyer be more economical.[46]

Additional problems plagued the case. Laidley informed Chase in April 1857 of a delay in interviewing witnesses because of bad weather, which had further slowed the pace of nineteenth century travel. Key witnesses in the case lived in Kentucky and Ohio, and because the winter had been very severe, it was spring before they could be interviewed.[47] That fall, Laidley reported that the case had finally been called, and he had learned of a new strategy on the part of the defense. They planned "the personal appearance of [the] eldest colored man who is twenty-one years of age, in open court who will direct the suit to be dismissed not desiring to have it prosecuted." Laidley explained, "The fact is the colored people are very much attached to Ratcliffe and his family."[48]

In February 1859, Chase's personal secretary, L.L. Rice, in a memo to the governor, expressed impatience with the case, which had by that time been pending in Virginia for six years. Rice placed part of the blame on the Ohio lawyer (whether he referred to Wilson or Laidley is unclear), "an old man who acknowledges himself superannuated." While the lawyer dawdled, Rice wrote, "those enslaved freemen are spending their best years in slavery." He closed with the opinion that, even though the state of Ohio had already spent more than three thousand dollars in prosecuting the suits, it was unlikely that the Virginia Pollys would ever return to freedom.[49]

Unfortunately, Rice was correct. In March, the case went to trial and was dismissed because the Pollys' freedom suit had been brought without their authorization. Apparently, kidnapped blacks and their white advocates—even when they included northern governors—were victims of a slave system that ensured that states' rights, slaveowners' prerogatives, and legal loopholes prevailed over justice and the widely acknowledged facts of such kidnapping cases as the Pollys'. [50]

But even this decision did not terminate activity in the case. In November 1859, Chase's secretary wrote to Ralph Leete, asking him to travel to Virginia to investigate and determine the possibility of continuing the case. [51] Leete agreed, adding that "the case in Virginia has been bungled and shamefully mismanaged from the commencement." He pointed out that the Kentucky cases, which he had prosecuted, had been successfully resolved, restoring the Pollys to their home. Despite his pessimism, Leete agreed to do all that he could to free the remaining members of the Polly family, because "the frequent visits from the mother of these children to make inquiries about them and her anguish, are enough to move any person of correct feeling to energetic action." [52]

The final results of the Peyton Polly case are unknown. As late as June 1860, Ralph Leete was still corresponding with Ohio officials about the case. Chase's successor, Governor William Dennison, urged Leete to continue his efforts on behalf of the Pollys, and Leete agreed to do so. [53] The case then disappears from the record. Given the lack of progress in the case over a decade, it is reasonable to assume that the state of Ohio was unsuccessful in trying to free the four Pollys enslaved in Virginia. Probably, they became free only with the advent of the Civil War.

What is especially interesting about the case is the presumed decision of the Virginia Pollys to remain in slavery. Although this may seem incomprehensible to modern readers, there are several possible explanations. One is that the Pollys were intimidated, either explicitly or implicitly, by their owner. Blacks who were uneducated may not have understood that the court proceeding was in their interest. Another possibility is one that underscores the theme of this work, the vulnerability that pervaded the lives of blacks. Perhaps the Pollys found a sense of security in slave life that they did not have as free people. Having lived most of their lives as slaves, both before and after being kidnapped, they may have seen freedom as an ambiguous, even frightening prospect. Since they knew firsthand how precarious freedom was, perhaps they chose not to risk it again. Without any known record of their feelings on the subject, one can only speculate.

Another question raised by this case is the motivation of the Ohio governors in helping the Polly family. As with Governor Seward in New York, Governor Mifflin in Pennsylvania, and Mayor Watson in Philadelphia, officials in Ohio put forth an extraordinary effort to assist a group of blacks. Not only was there no apparent political remuneration in terms of black votes, but assisting blacks could even have done harm to the careers of men dependent upon a racist electorate for their positions.

One possible reason for their behavior is that as officials of the government, they may have felt compelled to uphold the law, however unpopular. Kidnapping was illegal in most states. Regardless of these politicians' views of blacks and slavery, kidnapping was a crime, and as such, it imposed an obligation to fight it and to protect the citizens under the officials' jurisdiction. Beyond that, we know of the broader abolitionist stance of some of these officials, although little has been written about their antikidnapping work. Salmon Chase, for example, before becoming governor of Ohio, was known for his legal work on behalf of fugitive slaves. Seward, too, was a noted abolitionist. It is likely then, that these men believed in the immorality of slavery and, regardless of political expediency, were willing to fight to protect free blacks from enslavement.

Regardless of their individual motivations, officials who used the law to help free blacks escape illegal enslavement were the exception, not the norm. Most politicians simply ignored the pleas of kidnap victims. Politicians and private citizens who did help were consistently frustrated in their efforts to persuade state and federal officials to provide stronger protection for free black Americans against illegal enslavement. The attempt to force states to abolish their antiblack laws was disabled by the states' rights argument. The effort to enact a federal antikidnapping law was thwarted both by southern members of Congress who feared that any laws protecting blacks would interfere with their rights as slaveowners and by their racist northern sympathizers.

Even if all public officials had been inclined to apply the laws written to protect free blacks, numerous other laws served to encourage their enslavement. The federal fugitive slave laws, Negro seamen acts, and others described in chapter 2 show that in the main, the law was a foe, not a friend, to free blacks. Especially in the case of kidnapping, the law's unintentional facilitation of the crime revealed a deep-rooted hostility toward the free black population. Thus free blacks often found that the security some government officials tried to provide them under the law was not enough. They turned elsewhere in their fight against kidnapping and found stronger support from one group in particular, the abolitionists.

CHAPTER FOUR

"The Thought of Slavery Is Death to a Free Man": Abolitionist Response to Kidnapping

While government officials sometimes assisted victims of kidnapping, abolitionists were particularly dedicated to helping free blacks who were illegally enslaved. Abolitionist concern over kidnapping can be detected from the movement's very beginning, in the naming of its early organizations. The names they chose reveal a purpose much broader than simply the outlawing of slavery. The nation's first abolition society, formed by Philadelphia Quakers in 1775, initially called itself the Society for the Relief of Free Negroes Unlawfully Held in Bondage. In 1787 it was reorganized as the Pennsylvania Society for Promoting Abolition of Slavery, Relief of Free Negroes Held Illegally in Bondage, and for Improving the Condition of the African Race (hereafter referred to as PAS). The very fact that it remained in operation into the twentieth century, working mainly to improve black education, shows that the agenda of the Pennsylvania Abolition Society was far more encompassing than abolition alone.[1]

One of the initial goals of the PAS was the promotion of satellite organizations, which followed the naming pattern of the PAS.[2] In 1789, for example, the Maryland Society for Promoting the Abolition of Slavery, and for the Relief of Free Negroes and Others Held Unlawfully in Bondage was formed.[3] Similarly, the Delaware Society for Gradual Abolition, founded in 1788, reorganized in 1800 as the Delaware Society for Promoting the Abolition of Slavery and for the Relief and Protection of Free Blacks and People of Color Unlawfully Held in Bondage, or Otherwise Oppressed (hereafter DAS).[4]

Freeing blacks held illegally as slaves was an important goal for all of the early abolition societies.[5] "It must be assumed," Dwight Dumond has argued, "that anti-slavery societies or individuals initiated, provided the legal counsel for, and financed all cases involving the freedom of negroes."[6] The New York and New Jersey societies, for example, listed among their objectives the protection of free blacks and relief for those illegally enslaved.[7] Further south, the North Carolina Manumission Society addressed similar concerns in its early meetings.[8]

But the greatest effort by far in the fight against kidnapping came from the Delaware and Pennsylvania abolition societies.[9] As noted earlier, Delaware and Pennsylvania in particular witnessed a large number of kidnappings as a result of their large free black populations, proximity to the Mason-Dixon line (Delaware was a slave state), and ease of transportation to the South by way of the Delaware River, Delaware Bay, and adjacent coastal waters. These two organizations both witnessed and became involved in more kidnapping cases than any other abolition societies. Such cases were probably the largest single reason for the formation of the Delaware Abolition Society in 1788.[10] In its 1817 address to the American Convention of Abolition Societies, a loosely organized national body, the DAS asserted, "The state of Delaware forming a boundary line between the free and slave states is made the scene of frequent trade and frequent transgression of the rights of people of color. Men whom avarice had changed into demons either purchase blacks who owe a few years of service, or kidnap those who are free."[11]

The PAS also commended the work of the DAS, "placed as they are, in a situation where the detestable practice of kidnapping and stealing free Negroes is more prevalent perhaps than in any other state."[12] For this reason, the DAS tried, unsuccessfully, in 1802 to form a sister society on Maryland's Eastern Shore to replace the defunct Choptank Society, to aid the Delaware abolitionists, and to prosecute kidnappers in Maryland.[13] By 1817, however, the Philanthropic Society of Easton had organized on the Eastern

Shore, because, as it reported to the American Convention, "the practice of kidnapping free negroes has become so frequent in these parts."[14]

Pennsylvania, a free state "surrounded by slavery," also witnessed the frequent kidnapping of free blacks, and the PAS worked diligently to aid those illegally enslaved.[15] As W.E.B. Du Bois observed in his famous 1899 study, "Philadelphia was the natural gateway between the North and the South and for a long time there passed through it a stream of . . . kidnapped colored persons toward the South."[16] According to PAS member and chronicler Edward Needles, Quaker manumissions and the nation's first gradual abolition law in 1780 created a large free black population in Pennsylvania, which in turn attracted kidnappers. Cases of kidnapping became so numerous that people as individuals could no longer provide sufficient aid to the victims, and it was to meet this need that the Pennsylvania Abolition Society was mobilized.[17]

Quakers played an important part in the founding of the PAS and other abolition societies. Because of their commercial connections, American Quakers had frequent contact with British antislavery Quakers.[18] They were also influenced by the thinkers of the Enlightenment and the Great Awakening. The belief in rationalism and human rights, rather than in orginal sin, led the Quakers towards abolitionism. Quakers in America had actually begun discussing the abolition of slavery within their own community as early as 1688. By 1776, the Philadelphia Yearly Meeting, which included Friends from Pennsylvania, New Jersey, Delaware, and Maryland, prohibited the ownership of slaves by Quakers.[19] The majority of early abolitionists were Quakers, and they played an important role in the establishment of nearly all the early abolition societies except those in Connecticut and Kentucky. The national abolitionist body, the American Convention, was dominated by Quakers.[20] Of the twenty-four abolitionist conventions between 1794 and 1829, twenty met in Philadelphia, where the Quaker-controlled PAS was the largest and most active abolition society in the nation.[21] According to one recent scholar, "The gradualist . . . approach of Friends set the tone for the white antislavery movement in America from 1780 to 1833."[22]

Quakers were also fighting kidnapping at an early date. Olaudah Equiano (a.k.a. Gustavus Vassa), a black sailor who wrote his life story, witnessed numerous kidnappings, including some in Philadelphia. "If it were not for the benevolence of the Quakers in that city," he reported, "many of the sable race, who now breathe the air of liberty, would, I believe, be groaning indeed under some planter's chains."[23] There is evidence that some individual Quakers were drawn to the cause of abolition through early experiences with kidnapping victims. Among them was Thomas Garrett, the legendary Wilmington Underground Railroad conductor who had grown up on a farm outside Philadelphia. When a young black woman employed by his family was kidnapped, Garrett, then in his early twenties, pursued her assailants and vowed to devote his life to abolition.[24] Another conductor, North Carolina Quaker Levi Coffin, found that the first slave to whom he offered aid was actually a kidnapped freeman. At age fifteen, Coffin encountered a slave coffle at a neighbor's house. Upon speaking with the slaves, he learned that one of them, Stephen, had been kidnapped. Hired to drive sheep from his home in Philadelphia to Baltimore, Stephen had been seized upon arrival and taken to Virginia, where he was sold as a slave. Coffin later persuaded his father and several other Quakers to locate Stephen, who by then had been sold in Georgia. Eventually they managed to liberate him and return him to Philadelphia.[25]

The PAS and other abolitionist organizations helped curtail kidnapping through the compilation and publication of manumission records. The societies of Pennsylvania, Delaware, Maryland, Virginia, Choptank (Maryland), and Alexandria (Virginia) all examined county court records to ensure that manumissions were properly recorded, and they maintained their own accounts to preserve evidence that might be needed later in a kidnapping case or freedom suit.[26] The Delaware abolitionists went a step further when, in the summer of

1801, they began listing manumissions each month in the *Mirror of the Times and General Advertiser*, a Wilmington newspaper.[27] Despite such efforts, manumission records probably did not play a significant role in the battle against kidnapping. Consequently, in 1822 the Pennsylvania Society decided to record only those manumissions not already publicly listed, citing the expense and "the few instances in which the record has been useful."[28]

Abolitionists also pressured state governments to enact stronger antikidnapping laws and to enforce those already on the books. The Maryland Abolition Society, for example, petitioned its state legislature for more stringent antikidnapping laws in 1790, 1815, and again in 1816.[29] Similarly, the PAS decided to press state officials in Harrisburg in 1811 for a law to "prevent more effectively the practice of kidnapping Negroes within this Commonwealth" by imposing harsher penalties on kidnappers.[30] Later, Pennsylvania Society members met to draft a petition that argued that punishment under laws already enacted by the legislature was not strong enough to prevent the crime.[31] Asserting that "The soil of Pennsylvania having been frequently polluted by the footsteps of kidnappers," they sent a memorial to their legislators again in 1818.[32] The Pennsylvania legislature passed antikidnapping laws in 1820 and 1826, but the PAS remained dissatisfied and maintained the pressure for more protection against kidnapping; however, antikidnapping law was not strengthened until 1847.[33]

The DAS also frequently petitioned its state legislature for antikidnapping laws.[34] Although Delaware had passed such a law in 1793, it was considered ineffectual and was not well enforced.[35] Like its Pennsylvania counterpart, the DAS also experienced frustration in dealing with the legislature. In May of 1817, a DAS committee reported that, although it had collected signatures to petition the legislature in Dover for a strengthened antikidnapping law, the petition had never been introduced there. The committee expressed the belief that the petition had been purposely withheld by certain members of the legislature. A new PAS committee was formed to investigate the incident, including the determination of each member's vote on the antikidnapping bill, which had failed.[36] On July 4, that committee reported that the petition had been presented to Representative Nicholas G. Williamson and that two witnesses saw him deliver it to Representative Peter Vandever. The witnesses, fellow legislators Andrew Gray and George Clark, voted against the bill. Vandever, who voted for the bill, argued that Williamson had never given him the petition, adding that "no man feels a greater abhorrence [than I] at the practice [of kidnapping] and [I] would, as willingly as any other person, give any aid in my power to suppress the barbarous traffic in human flesh."[37] DAS committee member Edward Worrell confronted Williamson, charging that he, Gray, and Clark would not be reelected if their chicanery was made public. Williamson replied that he did not plan to run again and did not care what anyone thought of his opinion on the issue. He then left the room "with an air of great consequence, throwing defiance in the face of all concerned."[38] Later DAS appointed another committee to present petitions for an antikidnapping law and to do whatever else was deemed necessary to get the measure passed.[39] They continued the pressure, with numerous petitions to the legislature, but the law remained unaltered.[40]

One drawback to state laws against kidnapping was that they often went unenforced by state and local officials, particularly in slave states such as Delaware. Cambridge, Delaware, resident James Bryan accused his state legislature of having more interest in recovering fugitive slaves than in securing the freedom of kidnapping victims.[41] The major problem with state laws against kidnapping, however, was that they were of limited value in stopping a crime that involved interstate transportation. In most cases of kidnapping, a free black was abducted in a free state and taken into a slave state. Regardless of how stringent state antikidnapping laws were, and no matter how well state officials attempted to enforce them, they met with limited success because they needed cooperation from other states, usually southern. As noted earlier, the nation's first federal fugitive slave act resulted from problems Pennsylvania Governor Thomas Mifflin encountered in trying to prosecute three Virginia kidnappers. But while that incident culminated in a federal law to make interstate retrieval of runaway slaves easier, it did nothing to facilitate the prosecution of kidnappers.

Because of these legal hurdles, abolitionists also lobbied for the protection of free blacks on the national level. Quakers frequently sent memorials to the U.S. Congress complaining of the many free blacks held in bondage illegally. They requested that Congress make the laws more effective against kidnapping.[42] Government intervention against kidnapping was also a topic of concern at American Convention meetings. At its sixth annual meeting in 1799, officers of the Convention warned the abolition societies of the threat of kidnapping and urged their vigilance in stopping the "nefarious traffic."[43] The situation had evidently not improved by 1804, for the Convention then expressed the belief that a gang of kidnappers operated along the East Coast from Maine to Georgia, "like the vulture, soaring in apparent indifference, while watching for his prey."[44] A committee appointed to investigate kidnapping and the domestic slave trade issued a report at the 1827 meeting, which concluded that unless slavery itself was abolished, little could be done to quell the internal traffic, legal or otherwise, in human beings. Nevertheless, they continued to believe it was worthwhile for abolition societies to unite and memorialize Congress in an effort to stop the sale of slaves. The committee also stated that existing antikidnapping laws were sufficient to protect free blacks but that better enforcement was necessary.[45]

Abolitionists also appealed to the national government for assistance in individual cases of kidnapping. In 1788, the PAS wrote to Pennsylvania Governor Thomas Mifflin about John Davis, a free black resident of Washington County, in the southwestern part of the state. Davis had been kidnapped, taken to Virginia, and sold into slavery there. Three men had been indicted for the crime, but could not be tried because they had fled to Virginia. The PAS asked Mifflin to request that the Virginia governor extradite Davis and his kidnappers.[46]

In August 1791, Mifflin informed the state legislature of the PAS request and explained that the governor of Virginia had rejected the request for the extradition of the kidnappers, arguing that no law required him to comply.[47] With the help of President George Washington, Mifflin took his case to Congress, demanding enactment of a law that would expedite the recovery of criminals. Their efforts resulted in a law designed to return fugitives from justice (criminals), as well as fugitives from labor (runaways). The nation's first federal fugitive slave law, passed in 1793, had the ironic effect of facilitating not only the recovery of fugitive slaves, but also the kidnapping of free blacks, because it denied the accused the right to due process.[48]

Usually, abolition societies handled individual kidnapping cases without appealing to the government, and their involvement represented their most central role in the struggle to stamp out kidnapping. Reports from the American Convention of 1796 give a clear picture of the extent of abolitionist vigilance in "relieving persons unlawfully held in bondage":

New York - since January 1796
    90 complaints
    29 freed under a law prohibiting slave importation into state
    7 freed as free born (heavy damages recovered in some of these)
    2 unsuccessful
    21 pending
    19 under consideration
New Jersey
    many manumissions effected, no specific records
Pennsylvania
    many hundreds have been freed
Wilmington (Delaware)
    between 1788-1796 80 freed
Maryland
    many freed
Choptank (Maryland)
    between 1789-1796 60 freed, only 1 unsuccessful

Alexandria (Virginia)
    26 complaints
    6 freed under importation law
    5 expected to be freed
    14 pending, doubtful
Virginia
    20–30 suits pending

Although societies in Rhode Island, Connecticut, Washington, Delaware, Chestertown (Maryland), Wincester (Virginia), and Kentucky sent no accounts, this list reveals the number of cases that abolition societies considered, accepted, and successfully resolved.[49]

In addition to publicizing manumissions and lobbying state legislatures, abolitionists also helped in the recovery of kidnapping victims and in bringing their abductors to justice. A detailed examination of a few cases will illustrate the abolitionists' contribution to the antikidnapping crusade.

The case of Leah Roche came to the attention of the Delaware Abolition Society in 1803. When Roche was a child, her mother had placed her with Jacob Sellars of Wilmington, Delaware, and planned to indenture her to him if the arrangement proved suitable. But Roche's mother disappeared before the agreement was finalized. When Sellars died, Roche remained with his widow, who later married Thomas Cryer. In the spring of 1803, Cryer accused Roche of stealing two hundred dollars from him and had her jailed. Roche was tried and convicted of robbery, a crime that made her subject to sale into slavery under the law.[50]

Unable to pay her prosecution and jail fees, Roche remained incarcerated and was about to be sold for a term of seven years when Cryer paid her fees and took her away. Since the sheriff had offered Roche at a public sale as required by law, Cryer's payment did not give him a valid claim to her; legally, it was considered a loan. Cryer, however, regarded himself as Roche's legal master and hired her out to John Delaney of Newport, Delaware. From there, Roche was sold and taken to Havre de Grace, Maryland.[51]

The DAS Acting Committee discovered the young woman

at Havre de Grace, and "after considerable difficulty," pro-
cured her liberty and returned her to Wilmington. Her Maryland buyer, John McClatchy, found on an island in the Chesapeake Bay, admitted to trading twelve hundred dollars worth
of cattle for Roche, but claimed he believed the transaction
had been legal. The jailer in Newport acknowledged that
Cryer had taken Roche and stated that he had found her "a
good new master."[52]

The DAS regarded this as "conclusive evidence of the illegal intentions of Cryer and McClatchy" and began searching
for legal counsel and funding for prosecution. But the committee soon found itself in a predicament. Some committee
members and lawyers feared that if tried for kidnapping, the
two would be acquitted, since juries were unlikely to convict
whites of crimes committed against blacks. On the other
hand, the committee felt "much aversion" when their lawyer, George Read II, informed them that Cryer and Mc-
Clatchy were likely to be found guilty and would then be
sentenced to the punishment of whipping and cropping of
their ears. As they believed that mangling a person's body
served only to "debase rather than reform him," the committee decided to strike a deal and accepted one hundred
pounds from McClatchy and three hundred pounds from
Cryer, believing that this would deter future kidnappers.[53]

In 1802, the PAS took on a kidnapping case concerning
William Bachelor of Philadelphia, a free black man claimed
as a runaway slave. Two slave dealers, Joseph Ennells and a
Captain Frazier, arrested Bachelor and swore before a magistrate that he had been part of a slave gang in Maryland. Despite Bachelor's protests that he was free, Ennells and Frazier
obtained a certificate authorizing them to return the sup-
posed fugitive to Maryland. Fortunately for the victim, a Dr.
Kinley, whose family Bachelor had served, attempted to persuade the slave dealers that they had the wrong man. Failing
in this attempt, the doctor sought out Isaac Hopper of the
PAS and explained that his father had owned Bachelor but
had manumitted him.[54]

When Hopper pursued the kidnappers, Ennells drew his

pistol and announced that he had the magistrate's permission to take Bachelor. He threatened, "I will blow your brains out if you say another word on the subject." Hopper replied, "If thou were not a coward, thou wouldst not try to intimidate me with a pistol," and declared that he intended to prevent Bachelor's forced removal into Maryland. Bachelor exclaimed that he had never been in Maryland in his life and begged Hopper for help. "So your name is Hopper, is it?" asked Ennells. "I have heard of you. It's time the world was rid of you. You have done too much mischief already," accusing Hopper of depriving many slaveowners of their human property. "Thou art mistaken," Hopper responded, "I only prevent Southern marauders from robbing people of their liberty."[55]

Eventually, Hopper persuaded the kidnappers to return to the magistrate, this time with Kinley and other witnesses to attest to Bachelor's freedom, and the magistrate ordered him released. Hopper then set about arranging for the prosecution of the kidnappers. When he arrived at Ennells's lodging with a warrant and two officers, Ennells threatened to shoot them. Ennells eventually surrendered, although at one point he hit one of the officers across the face with his cane. He was bound over to the next mayor's court. The defendant's lawyers then tried to persuade Hopper to drop the matter. He replied that it was no longer in his hands, but rather those of the PAS. In the words of Hopper's biographer, Lydia Maria Child, the PAS "had commenced the prosecution with no vindictive feelings, but merely with the view of teaching people to be careful how they infringed upon the rights of free men." When Ennells agreed to pay all costs, the PAS allowed the charges against him to be dropped.[56]

These two cases illustrate one of the gravest realities abolitionists faced in the fight against kidnapping. Even when a kidnapper was caught and successfully prosecuted by abolition societies, they often accepted a cash settlement from the defendant(s). The societies could hardly have acted otherwise, and it is possible that the greatest service they accorded kidnapped free people was financial assistance. When held as suspected fugitives, blacks faced not only the hazards of incarceration, but also court costs and lawyers' fees, as well as transportation costs for witnesses, and most blacks, living in poverty, had little hope of release even when they could prove their free status. The bulk of these debts were borne directly or indirectly by the abolitionists. For example, John Brown, a free man jailed in Portsmouth, Virginia, was about to be sold into slavery when the PAS paid his jail fees.[57] The PAS also paid for some of the expenses of Delawarian John Kollock, who wrote asking the society to help with the costs of returning two kidnapped boys to their home in Philadelphia.[58]

Numerous incidents such as these placed an extreme burden on abolition societies. As early as 1798, the Richmond Abolition Society lamented to the American Convention that society funds were insufficient to provide proper relief to kidnapping victims.[59] In their address to the American Convention of 1817, DAS members expressed the hope that recent convictions of kidnappers would serve as a deterrent, but admitted that the problem would continue because of the lack of sufficient funds for prosecution.[60] At a meeting in 1794, the PAS had discussed the possibility of granting funds to the DAS to help its "extraordinary efforts" to aid kidnapping victims, by 1821 the PAS conceded that it no longer had the financial resources even to handle all of the cases that came to its own attention.[61] The willingness of the abolition societies to drop charges if kidnappers paid fines and court costs was a reflection of this financial burden.

In addition to insufficient funding, there were other factors which prevented the successful resolution of kidnapping cases. A legal system that placed the burden of proof upon the victim, the difficulty of proving a black person's free status without the testimony of black witnesses (which in most states was not permissible evidence against a white defendant), and extreme racism and hostility toward free blacks often proved to be hurdles even the most tireless abolitionist failed to overcome. The sheer number of kidnapping cases alone was daunting. At the American Convention of 1800, the Virginia Abolition Society reported that because it was involved in lawsuits for nearly one hundred individuals, it was unable to prosecute all the cases adequately.[62]

Inevitably, abolitionists did not triumph in every kidnapping case they entered. One unsuccessful case was that of a woman known only as Henrietta, a Delaware indentured servant jailed in Georgia and about to be sold as a slave. As of November 1817, the DAS was informed that several people in Georgia had filed a petition on her behalf to prevent the sale. They needed a witness from Delaware to identify her and return her to Delaware if released. Even though justice seemed imminent in this case, the DAS reported in July 1818 that it had given up on the case.[63]

Another unsuccessful case was that of Elijah Morris, bound out to Warner Mifflin, Jr., a founding member of the DAS and one of its representatives at the first American Convention.[64] Mifflin had placed Morris with Charles Hazzard, captain of a small sloop on the Delaware River. Hazzard sold Morris as a slave in Tennessee. When Morris and several others heard that they were going to be sold into the Deep South, they escaped. The men were soon caught and jailed and were about to be taken to Natchez when their Tennessee jailer wrote to Mifflin to ask if Morris was actually a free man. If so, he asked that Mifflin send proof, "as the thought of slavery is death to a free man." Joseph Christy of Fredericksburg, Maryland, was hired to represent Morris, but as he explained in a letter to Mifflin's brother Daniel, the case was difficult because he could not positively prove that the victim was Elijah Morris. He closed the letter saying, "I am sorry justice cannot be obtained in this matter."[65]

In some kidnapping cases, the final disposition remains unknown because the victim's name has simply disappeared from abolition society records. The narrative of Philip Johnston was recorded in New Orleans in September of 1788 and was read to the PAS Acting Committee that December. Johnston, a slave in Louisiana, claimed that his mother was a freeborn woman and that he therefore was free. At the age of eleven, he had been apprenticed to a Mr. Taylor of Philadelphia and in May 1787 sailed on board the *Molly* from Philadelphia. Bound for Saint Croix, the ship put in for provisions at Cap Francois, on Haiti's northern coast, after fifty-three days. There Johnston was told by the captain, Benjamin Crawford, to go with two men, who took him to jail, where he remained imprisoned for three weeks without explanation. Then he was released and taken to New Orleans as a slave, having been sold by the captain. Hearing Johnston's tale, his master took Johnston to the governor of Louisiana, who agreed to look into the case.[66]

The PAS Acting Committee agreed to investigate and by its next meeting had obtained a statement from Johnston's sister Ruth, who affirmed his freedom. Testimony from Henry Haines, who had sailed with Johnston, confirmed Captain Crawford's attempt to sell him in Savannah. Minutes of the committee meetings throughout 1789 referred to Johnston's case as still active, but after that no further references to the case appear. In March 1789, Pennsylvania Governor Thomas Mifflin requested help from Spanish authorities in New Orleans to liberate Johnston. But the fate of Philip Johnston remains a mystery.[67]

These cases, which illustrate the multitude of kidnappings with which abolitionists concerned themselves, occurred between 1788 and 1818. One of the most striking features of abolitionist support of the antikidnapping cause was that it did not remain constant throughout the pre-Civil War period. After the 1820s, the abolitionists' resistance to kidnapping declined noticeably. This was not the result of a decrease in the number of kidnappings, for they continued to rise throughout the antebellum period, particularly after the passage of the Fugitive Slave Law of 1850.

The persistence of kidnappers was noted by many. Abolitionist and newspaper editor Hezekiah Niles warned in 1826, "This most abominable trade of all trades has been much revived of late. . . . The stealing of children is frequent. We have accounts of numerous cases; and generally, the trade in *human beings* is lively."[68] In 1842, abolitionist and former slaveholder James G. Birney reported, "Kidnapping is carried on in this country to a great extent—in some parts of it, almost without the necessity of secrecy or concealment. Scores of unsuspecting colored persons, born free, are annually spirited away from the free States, and sold into slavery in the South."[69] The *Liberator* estimated the number of kidnappings between 1831 and 1860 at nearly one hundred, although as Winfield Collins later noted, "The number detected probably bears little relation to the number actually kidnapped."[70]

Despite the recurring crime, the records of the most vigilant abolition society in the antikidnapping battle, the PAS, reveal a marked decrease in activity against kidnapping in the 1820s. DAS Acting Committee records are not available after 1819, but the society's chronicler, Monte Calvert, stated that the society had become more active in writing antislavery petitions and essays than in attending to individual cases of kidnapping.[71]

Why did abolitionists abandon the issue of kidnapping? The best way to understand this change in attitude is to examine the change within the abolition movement itself. The gradualist approach of the Quakers had set the tone for the movement through the first quarter of the nineteenth century.[72] Though gradual abolitionists disagreed with laws that legitimized slavery and labored to change them, most continued to work within the law. Until slavery was completely eradicated, gradual abolitionists worked within the system to keep as many people out of slavery as possible. The report of the New York Manumission Society to the American Convention meeting in 1809 embodied this attitude: "As on the one hand we should suffer no one to linger in slavery whom the laws have pronounced free, so on the other we should never outstrip the laws by making inroads into private right, or improperly interrupting domestic tranquility. Hence the first object is to give perfection to our statutes regulating slavery, and the next to see their emancipating provisions strictly and equitably enforced."[73]

Changes occurring in the nation at this time, however, contributed to abolitionists' abandonment of this position. During the first quarter of the nineteenth century, the United States was becoming increasingly oriented toward expansion, geographical and material. According to James Brewer Stewart, "The cosmopolitan forces of economic interdependence, urbanization, democratic politics, and mass communication all posed major challenges to provincial New England culture." The massive religious revival at the same time and its attendant reform movements provided a means to reassert traditional New England culture in a rapidly changing world. The momentum created by the revival brought many converts into reform causes, particularly abolition. Their new religious fervor led this generation of abolitionists to view slavery as a sin, and thus they had no patience for gradual abolition. They embodied instead a desire for immediate and total emancipation.[74]

Their lack of moderation led many immediatists to make no distinction between legal enslavement and illegal kidnapping of free people. Because they believed slavery to be morally reprehensible under any circumstances, immediatists often refused to respect any laws that acknowledged the rights of slaveowners to human property. "An Incendiary Fanatic" argued in the *Liberator*, "Every native of the United States was born free. The slave must have been kidnapped; therefore the holder of that slave is a Man-Stealer, or an accessory, or a receiver of stolen goods, or a purchaser of a human being whom he knew was stolen."[75] Frederick Douglass echoed this feeling, referring to all slave catchers as kidnappers. By the early 1850s, he even went so far as to reverse his earlier nonviolent stance, arguing that such individuals had given up their right to live.[76] The refusal of abolitionists to accept the practical distinction between legal enslavement and illegal kidnapping was reflected not only in word, but also in deed, as evidenced by the Underground Railroad and by such "rescues" of fugitives as the celebrated "Jerry case" of Schenectady, New York, and the Oberlin-Wellington rescue.[77]

The gradualists, however, had lived in a world that was not being torn apart by slavery, so they could afford to be patient. They witnessed signs that made them optimistic that slavery could be eradicated. Following the late eighteenth century achievement of abolition in the North, gradualists had reason to believe that success in the South would soon follow. They believed that over time "moral suasion" would triumph in the South and that eventually southerners would enact gradual abolition laws like those passed in the northern states. Gradual abolitionists, however, failed to realize the depth to which slavery had become intertwined with southern culture and economic progress, especially with the headlong rush to expand into the West and Southwest. To gradualists, emancipation in the North and the end of the international slave trade represented a most encouraging trend. As Winthrop Jordan has pointed out, these gains "salved the nation's conscience that *something* was being done about slavery."[78]

Despite such promising advances, several events in the early nineteenth century contributed to the growth and expansion, rather than the destruction, of slavery. The invention of the cotton gin led to the spread of cotton production in the Deep South. Development of the Southwest opened the way for extension of the cotton empire and slavery along with it. As slave prices rose accordingly, the internal slave trade flourished. According to Winthrop Jordan, "A reaction set in, and by 1807, abolition of slavery in the Upper South seemed a much dimmer prospect than it had in 1790."[79]

A new solution to the slavery issue appeared at this time as well. After the formation of the American Colonization Society in 1816, gradual abolitionist sentiment was easily rechanneled into colonization. Colonization had great appeal as a solution to the problem of slavery without challenging American racism. The American Colonization Society helped inform the public about the plight of free blacks, but this had a partially negative effect. By continually emphasizing the degradation of free blacks, colonizationists may have contributed to increased racism.[80]

Racism may have been a motivating factor in the abolitionists' withdrawal from their embrace of the multifaceted

approach to abolishing slavery. Their defection in the antebellum period must be understood against the backdrop of
increased racism manifested in America. Historians have her-
alded Andrew Jackson's presidency as the "Age of the Common Man," a time in which Americans discarded traditional
concepts of social stratification. The strongest evidence of
this was the adoption of nearly universal white male suf-
frage. Free black men were excluded from this expansion of
democracy, and the few who had previously enjoyed the
franchise were deprived of that right. Free black men had
been legally entitled to vote throughout the North during
the colonial and Revolutionary eras, although many were
prevented from exercising that right by local custom. In the
nineteenth century, however, states began disenfranchising
their black residents, often as the vote was extended to all
white men. New states entering the Union after 1820 also
excluded blacks from the franchise. By 1840, black men in
only four New England states could vote on an equal basis
with white men.[81] As Merton L. Dillon has noted, "Jacksonian democracy represented, among other things, obedience
to popular will. In the South, popular will generally supported slavery; in the North it tolerated the debasement of
the free Negro."[82]

Some of this increasing prejudice against free blacks was a
result of their growing numbers.[83] On the eve of the Revolutionary War, about four thousand slaves and several hundred
free blacks lived in the northern ports of Philadelphia, New
York, and Boston. Fifty years later, only a handful of slaves
remained, mostly in New York, while the free black population had swelled to approximately twenty-two thousand.[84]

As the free black population increased, so did numbers of
Irish immigrants, and these two groups frequently came into
conflict. Competition for jobs was fierce between black and
Irish workers, but the roots of American racism certainly
predate Irish immigration, and job discrimination against
blacks was present long before the Irish arrived. However,
the migration of large numbers of Irish, another destitute
people grappling for a rung on the economic ladder, only

exacerbated the problem.[85] The Irish quickly became associated with the Democrats, a party with an established tradition of racism. Led by defenders of slavery such as John C. Calhoun, who pressed southern economic interests in the tariff controversy of 1828, the Democrats were already entrenched in their antiblack posture by the time massive migration of immigrants began.[86]

Thus, by the antebellum period abolitionists were fighting an ever-increasing tide of racism. Philadelphia in particular represents a fascinating study of the intersection of abolitionism and racism. Because of its location along the Mason-Dixon line, as well as the Quakers' practice of manumitting their slaves and the state's passage of the nation's first abolition law, Pennsylvania had gained a large free black population. Philadelphia had seen the birth of both the abolition movement and the most active and powerful abolition society in the early National period. Philip Foner has argued, however, that "Philadelphia was also the most anti-Negro city of the North and the most rigidly segregated metropolis above the Mason-Dixon line."[87] Comments from both white and black visitors to the city support Foner's assertion. British traveler Alexander Majoribanks, for example, called Philadelphia America's most racist city.[88] Black abolitionist and author William Wells Brown agreed, claiming, "Colorphobia is more rampant here than in the pro-slavery, negro-hating city of New York."[89]

The apparent contradiction is not inexplicable. Throughout the pre-Civil War period, Philadelphia was home to one of the country's largest free black communities.[90] The population had increased as a result of both legal and illegal southern migration, and often free blacks came into direct competition with whites for jobs, particularly with the growing body of Irish immigrants.[91] Blacks were on the losing end of this battle, and the result was extreme poverty in the city's black community. Even worse, blacks suffered much violence at the hands of whites. Philadelphia was the site of at least six major antiblack riots in the 1830s and 1840s, as well as a score of minor skirmishes.[92] In the midst of the riots, delegates at the 1837–38 Pennsylvania constitutional convention succeeded in depriving the state's black men of the franchise.[93] White residents in southern Pennsylvania had agitated persistently to get a bill through the legislature that would have limited black migration, but they were blocked at every turn by state Representative Thaddeus Stevens.[94] In 1911, Edward Turner summed up the complexity of black-white relations in Pennsylvania and also explained the eventual change in focus of the abolition movement: "They have no love for the black man free . . . [although] they pitied him as a slave."[95]

More practical concerns may have ultimately played the most important role in the abolitionists' abandonment of kidnapped free blacks. By the 1820s, their societies were increasingly suffering from lack of funds. Court costs, lawyers' fees, and jail fees placed a severe burden on kidnap victims. As the number of kidnappings increased, abolitionists may have simply given up in the face of an overwhelming financial burden. They may have come to believe that focusing all their efforts on ending slavery was the best tactic in the long run. Certainly, total abolition would have brought about an end to kidnapping. In the meantime, though, victims of kidnapping lost a valuable ally when abolitionists refocused their attention. Without abolitionist assistance, free blacks organized within their own communities and vowed to defend themselves against kidnappers.

CHAPTER FIVE

"An Almost Sleepless Vigilance": Black Resistance to Kidnapping

Despite the strenuous efforts of government officials and abolitionists on behalf of kidnapped free blacks, the black community and many kidnapping victims came to the realization that they must ultimately rely upon themselves. The struggle of whites to release individuals held illegally in slavery and to gain legal protection for free blacks was admirable. Particularly surprising were the endeavors of a few southerners who risked their own lives when aiding a free black person. Nevertheless, whites could afford to relax in their struggle against kidnapping—and often did so—as it was superceded by the larger sectional controversy. Blacks, however, could not abandon the fight against kidnapping because it was for them an everyday fact of life. Along the Mason-Dixon line, resistance to kidnapping was an inseparable part of the daily struggle for survival. Blacks continued the battle during the antebellum period, attempting to fill the void left by the abolitionists' desertion. Much of black resistance to kidnapping was spontaneous, but blacks also organized at the local, state, and national levels to bring an end to this threat to their community.

The impediments to black resistance were great. The small pool of jobs customarily available to blacks was reduced by immigrant competition. Inferior segregated schools (when the state provided any form of education) further hindered black aspirations. Without black voting power, political parties and elected officals found it easy to ignore the demands of their black constituents. Racism pervaded the legal system, the government, even the abolition movement, ultimately forcing blacks to rely upon themselves, incidental assistance notwithstanding. What Gary B. Nash has noted about the black community in Philadelphia was true for blacks throughout America: "From the beginning free black Philadelphians understood that the only secure foundation upon which to fashion their lives was one of being a people within a people and relying on their own resources rather than white benevolence."[1]

To some degree, racism explains the difficulty of uncovering black sources on this topic. While the white, upper-class Pennsylvania Abolition Society members had both time and money to spend in working on the problem of kidnapping and recording their efforts, blacks had neither. Thus, black vigilance no doubt exceeds the written record of such activities. James and Lois Horton have observed that members of Boston's black vigilance committee tended to be skilled workers and professionals. Such membership was unusual, however, as "the majority of blacks—especially poor blacks—involved in aiding fugitive slaves worked in informal all-black groups." Such groups often formed in response to a particular incident and afterward disbanded.[2] Permanent organization was unnecessary; since members of the community lived so closely together and maintained daily contact with each other, they could immediately regroup and take action when threatened. It is reasonable to expect that the same was true of antikidnapping activity.

Most recorded examples of black organization come from the large eastern port cities of Boston, New York, and Philadelphia. These cities had large black populations, as well as facilities such as churches that made it easier for them to organize. Initially kept out of most white-run abolition societies, blacks in cities formed their own groups, frequently banding together to assist fugitive slaves who were attracted to urban anonymity. Although the intense reaction to the Fugitive Slave Law of 1850 is well-known, urban blacks had earlier developed both formal and informal ways of assisting both fugitives and free blacks. As early as 1819, for example, blacks formed the Baltimore Society for the Protection of Free People of Color. Vigilance committees followed in New

York, Boston, and Philadelphia. Informal interracial net-
works were also in operation in some cities, both before and
after the organization of the vigilance committees.[3]

Boston, in particular, had a long history of black organization for self-defense. An interracial, black-led Committee
of Vigilance had formed in the city in 1846 to help fugitives,
and a large segment of Boston's black population was active
in aiding fugitive slaves. Black Bostonians had also organized
to protest the Negro seamen acts. Although black sailors resided in ports all along the East Coast, Boston housed the
largest number of them. About 20 percent of black workers
in antebellum Boston were in fact seamen.[4]

But the black response to kidnapping predated even these
examples of black activism. In February 1788, Boston blacks
led by Prince Hall petitioned the Massachusetts legislature for
justice in an incident of kidnapping. Early that month, three
black men had been lured aboard a ship in the city's harbor. A
Connecticut man named Avery and an accomplice shackled
the three, and the ship set sail for the Caribbean island of
Martinique.[5] Although the incident caused outrage among
both whites and blacks in the city, it was one of Boston's leading black citizens, Prince Hall, who took the initiative. Hall,
probably best-known for founding the Black Masonic Lodge,
was also a Methodist minister and a Revolutionary War veter-
an.[6] He and the other memorialists argued that not only was
the kidnapping reprehensible in and of itself, but it had also
caused grave concern about the security of everyone in the free
black community. "What then are our lives and Lebeties [*sic*]
worth if they may be taken a way in shuch [*sic*] a cruel and
injust manner as these," the petitioners demanded. Because
free black sailors had been sold as slaves, there were many in
the city who would not work at their trades for fear of being
stolen away.[7]

Supporting Hall's petition was another one written by
Reverend Jeremy Belknap and signed by ninety ministers. A
group of Quakers sent their own statement to the legislature.
Responding to this pressure, the Massachusetts legislature
enacted a law in March 1788 that prohibited the slave trade

and provided financial compensation for kidnapping victims and their families. This new law was added to an antikidnapping law that was previously in effect in the state.[8] In April, word was received that the victims had been sold in Martinique but had insisted on their free status and refused to work. Massachusetts Governor John Hancock obtained their release, and they returned home.[9]

Boston's free blacks also turned to the national government for redress against their enslavement. In 1843, 150 black Bostonians, including several shipowners, asked Congress to provide relief to free black sailors who were being jailed in southern ports, at the risk of being sold as slaves. The Committee on Commerce made a very favorable report on the petition, stating, "Probably no paper was ever addressed to the Congress of the United States, which represented more of the intelligence, virtue, patriotism, and property also, of the metropolis of New England." The committee concluded that the Negro seamen acts should be repealed, but added that Congress had no authority to do so. By publishing a series of resolutions against the laws and various other documents relevant to the case, it hoped to influence both the states that had such laws and the federal judiciary to take action against the Negro seamen acts.[10]

Philadelphia's black population had expressed its concerns over kidnapping to the national government even earlier than blacks in Boston. Philadelphia, as noted earlier, was a center of kidnapping because of its location along the Delaware River, close to slave states Delaware and Maryland. The city also had one of the nation's largest and best-organized free black communities. As Gary Nash has noted, "For two generations after the Revolution, Philadelphia was the largest and most important center of free black life in the United States." In the spring of 1787, leaders including Richard Allen, founder and bishop of the African Methodist Episcopal Church, and fellow minister Absalom Jones formed the Free African Society, which may have been the first black benevolent society in the United States.[11] The organization's initial purpose was social, but within several years members had turned their attention to antislavery work, including the prevention of kidnapping. [12]

Early in 1800, Allen, Jones, and others sent a petition to the U.S. Congress, urging that the federal government address the issue of kidnapping. Their detailed depiction of how kidnapping was accomplished demonstrated that they had firsthand knowledge of the problem. In fact, Allen himself had nearly fallen victim to this villainy. Born a slave on the Delaware plantation of Philadelphia lawyer Benjamin Chew, Allen eventually purchased his freedom and moved to Philadelphia. One day, Allen was confronted by a Maryland slaveowner who accused him of being a slave who had escaped four years earlier. At that time Allen had been a resident of Philadelphia for two decades; even the magistrate assigned to the case knew this and was embarrassed by the obvious case of mistaken identity. When the slaveowner refused to admit his mistake and cursed the judge, Allen was immediately released. [13]

What followed showed the twists of irony that frequently mark American race relations. Allen decided to sue for false arrest. With well-known Philadelphia abolitionist Isaac Hopper as his lawyer, Allen won a settlement of eight hundred dollars. Unable to pay, the kidnapper was jailed as a debtor for three months, after which Allen engineered his release; Allen felt that the slaveowner "had suffered enough to deter him from taking up free people again." [14] Despite the positive outcome, this incident aptly illustrates the pervasive vulnerability of free black Americans. What hope could the average person of color have for safety when even an esteemed figure such as Richard Allen could be assaulted in the street? As Allen's biographer, Carol George, has indicated, as long as slavery existed, free blacks were not secure: "The freeman's future was inexorably linked to the peculiar institution, and even if a man became a bishop, as Allen did, he was constantly reminded of just how tenuous his situation really was." [15]

Allen, Jones, and fellow-signatories of the Philadelphia petition had a very personal stake in the issue of kidnapping.

Knowing that most members of Congress had little sympathy for blacks, the seventy-three black memorialists tried to place the problem of kidnapping in the widest possible context. Not only was kidnapping a violation of the Constitution, they stated, but it was morally wrong as well: "Can any Commerce, Trade or transaction so detestably shock the feelings of Man, or degrade the dignity of his nature equal to this, and how increasingly is the evil aggravated when practised in a Land, high in profession of the benign doctrines of our blessed Lord, who taught his followers to do unto others as they would they should do unto them!"[16]

A spirited debate ensued in the House after Pennsylvania Representative Robert Waln's presentation of the petition. Much of the opposition grew out of the question of whether or not Congress had jurisdiction over kidnapping. But other issues intruded as well, and it soon became evident that blacks could not readily expect support from northern lawmakers. Harrison Otis of Massachusetts, for one, had no patience with the black memorialists. He claimed that they were simply the foils of abolitionists and did not even know what was written in the petition, much less understand it. The memorial could set a dangerous precedent, he cautioned, because "it would teach them [blacks] the art of assembling together, debating, and the like, and would soon, if encouraged, extend from one end of the Union to the other." John Brown of Rhode Island added his name to the racist attack when he said that he supported slavery and that slaves who moved North had come only "to reside as vagabonds and thieves."[17]

Blacks were not the only target of this attack, for their white supporters were also assailed. Seeking an earlier version of the famous "gag rule," Virginian John Randolph urged the House to ban the introduction of similar petitions in the future. This was an unsuccessful attempt to silence the Quakers, who frequently petitioned Congress on the subject of slavery and the condition of free blacks. It is apparent from this and subsequent debates that the Quakers, who were referred to by Representative Robert Goodloe Harper of South Carolina as "a religious body whose fanaticism leads them to think it a bounden duty to come to the House every year," were a thorn in the side of many in Congress. At least one representative, George Thatcher of Massachusetts, defended the Quakers, arguing that "wherever there was a humane or benevolent institution, the Quakers were at the bottom of it . . . they deserved little of the odium which had been lavished on them."[18]

The House appointed a committee to investigate the blacks' petition. This body agreed with the petitioners that there was "a very considerable Trade" in which "many Blacks and People of Colour entitled to their Freedom . . . are under cover of the Fugitive Law entrapped, kidnapped, and carried off." The committee recommended that the Fugitive Slave Law of 1793 be amended to prevent more effectively the kidnapping of free blacks. It suggested a more adequate examination of suspected slaves and a requirement that all ships' captains transporting captured fugitives south carry a justice's statement attesting that those being transported were indeed slaves.[19] While Congress apparently did not act on the committee's recommendations, the petition had, ironically, opened the door for revision of the fugitive law. Several Congressmen expressed a desire to strengthen it, and a year after the petition had been presented, a bill to impose a harsher penalty on those harboring or employing fugitive slaves was voted down in the House. Southerners thus nearly managed to turn to their own advantage an attempt to assist free blacks.[20]

Blacks also petitioned the federal government for redress against a lesser-known law that had the same effect as the fugitive slave law: rendering free people slaves. The earliest known black petition to Congress dealt with a case of rescinded manumission in North Carolina. In 1797, four black men complained that even though they had been declared free in court, the state legislature had passed a law that resulted in their being remanded to slavery. Apparently they had been emancipated in 1776, contrary to a law passed the previous year prohibiting manumission except in cases of meritorious service and then only through the county courts or legislature. In 1777, the prohibition on manumission was reinforced, and the legislature authorized the seizure and sale of manumitted slaves.[21]

Although the four petitioners had managed to escape to freedom (their memorial was sent from Philadelphia), they mentioned family members and others still held illegally in slavery in North Carolina. Their petition was hotly debated in the House, the main objections coming from southern representatives who argued that it was not an issue appropriate for discussion by the federal legislature. States' rights theory dictated that the issue was for the state of North Carolina to decide. James Madison suggested that if the four men were indeed free, they should apply to North Carolina's Court of Appeals for relief. The House voted not to receive the petition.[22]

The issue involved more than the four men who wrote from Philadelphia. In a memorial to Congress in 1798, a group of Quakers asked for the same assistance. According to the petitioners, a group of North Carolina Quakers from Perquimans and Pasquotank counties had emancipated fifty-six of their slaves in 1776. According to the 1777 law, the Perquimans and Pasquotank county courts ordered the sale of a large number of free people. In 1778, several of these cases were brought before the Superior Court of the Edenton District, where the decision was reversed on the grounds that the county courts had exceeded their jurisdiction and violated the Bill of Rights. Some of the manumitted slaves had been set free, but after the legislature again reinforced the ban on manumission in 1796, 144 were "reduced into cruel bondage under the existing or retrospective laws." An argument ensued in Congress over whether to permit a second reading of the Quaker memorial. A committee formed to investigate met with the Quakers to obtain more facts. The committee then reported that the case was a judicial rather than a legislative question, and the memorial was dismissed.[23]

Like Philadelphia, New York City was the scene of black antikidnapping initiative. In September 1850, William Powell, secretary of the Manhattan Anti-Slavery Society and proprietor of the Colored Seamen's Home, visited New York City Mayor C.S. Woodhull to request that the city protect free blacks from kidnapping. For years, Powell had been an activist for black sailors, working especially to publicize the plight of black seamen imprisoned under the Negro seamen acts.[24] In 1850, Powell wondered what guarantee blacks could expect against false arrest under the Fugitive Slave Law. He referred to "the peculiar position we [free blacks] occupy in this state—depending upon the magistery of the People of New York to defend her citizens." The mayor, however, gave blacks little support when he stated that city officials had been prohibited from carrying out the federal law and that he could offer free people no advice on how to protect themselves from kidnapping.[25]

Fifteen years earlier, the lack of government support had led New York blacks to organize for their own defense. The New York Committee of Vigilance was, as Benjamin Quarles has termed it, "the greatest" of the antebellum black self-defense organizations.[26] It was particularly active in the fight against kidnapping. As with other vigilance committees, one purpose was to provide assistance to fugitive slaves, and the New York City organization helped hundreds, including Frederick Douglass.[27] But the primary reason for forming the group may have been antikidnapping work. At its first meeting, members discussed organizing "for the purpose of adopting measures to ascertain, if possible, the extent to which the cruel practice of kidnapping men, women and children, is carried on in this city, and to aid such unfortunate persons as may be in danger of being *reduced to Slavery.*"[28] Although the organization, like a similar one in Philadelphia, was interracial, it was run largely by blacks.[29]

The New York Vigilance Committee was founded and led by David Ruggles. Born in Norwich, Connecticut, Ruggles moved to New York City as a young man and began a career in antislavery work. He worked as an agent for a New York abolitionist newspaper, the *Emancipator,* and independently as an abolition lecturer and author. His duties as secretary of the committee included investigating kidnapping cases. Ruggles interviewed black victims, as well as whites who were holding blacks illegally in slavery, and he acted as an advocate in court for kidnapped free blacks and suspected fugitives.[30]

Ruggles often came into conflict with kidnappers, slaveholders, and others who exhibited hostility toward him. In one instance, which Ruggles detailed in a letter published in the *New York American,* he himself was almost the victim of an attempted kidnapping. Because of his involvement in the arrest of the captain of a slave ship in New York harbor, several men came to Ruggles's home and attempted to seize him, but he managed to escape. "Now whether these men did *intend* to take me from my bed and to the South . . . or to 'put an end to my existence,' if I *resisted*," Ruggles wrote, "I cannot say in the absence of proof; I hope they did not." He claimed that there had been "a conspiracy on foot to kidnap and to sacrifice me upon the altar of slavery."[31] Nor was this an isolated incident. At a meeting of the New York Vigilance Committee several years later, one of Ruggles's associates, Augustus W. Hanson, revealed another plot to kidnap the secretary. Hanson said that a New York magistrate had offered fifty thousand dollars to anyone who would abduct Ruggles and take him into the South.[32] This report confirmed the belief of members at the first committee meeting that kidnapping represented a serious threat to the black community: "We have found the practice so extensive that no colored man is safe."[33]

The vigilance committees have been characterized by Jane and William Pease as fighting only individual cases of kidnapping, "rather than underlying issues." Yet Robert Purvis, leader of the Philadelphia organization, called his group "a formidable obstacle" to kidnappers.[34] Although the organizations indeed focused on aid to individual kidnapped free blacks and fugitives, certainly their very existence challenged the system of white domination, a crucial role. Free blacks were determined to defend themselves in the face of white aggression. The mainly black and black-led vigilance committees are solid evidence of this determination.

Free blacks who tried to work with their local, state, and federal governments to gain better protection for blacks under the law illustrated one response to kidnapping in the black community. Other blacks however, made no distinction between kidnappers who broke the law and slave catchers who abided by it.[35] Philadelphia's vigilance committee was formed, according to black abolitionist member William Still, in reaction to the Fugitive Slave Law of 1850 (although an earlier organization in the city dated from 1837). "In this dark hour," Still wrote in his 1872 book on the Underground Railroad, "when colored men's rights were so insecure, as a matter of self-defense, they felt called upon to arm themselves and resist all kidnapping intruders, although clothed with the authority of the wicked law."[36]

Frederick Douglass expressed similar convictions. He referred to both legal slave catchers and illegal kidnappers when he noted among the black population of New Bedford, Massachusetts, "a determination to protect each other from the blood-thirsty kidnapper, at all hazards."[37] In an editorial in *Frederick Douglass' Paper* entitled "Is It Right and Wise to Kill a Kidnapper?" Douglass again made no distinction between the two activities. Writing about the case of Anthony Burns, a fugitive slave captured in Boston and returned to the South in a famous 1854 public confrontation, Douglass declared that "when James Batchelder [who died trying to stop a mob from freeing Burns from jail] . . . took upon himself the revolting business of a kidnapper . . . he had forfeited his right to live."[38]

The linkage of illegal kidnappers and legal slave catchers was based not only on black perception, but also upon reality. Black self-defense groups organized in response to gangs who attacked both slaves and free blacks. A "gang of cut-throats" known as the Blackbirders, for example, kidnapped free blacks and fugitives in the notorious Five Points district of New York City. In 1829, the young Henry Highland Garnet encountered the Blackbirders when they abducted his sister Eliza. Although the Garnets were fugitives, the gang had no authority to take them, and the Garnets had the gang successfully prosecuted.[39]

William Parker and his neighbors in southeastern Pennsylvania responded to a similar threat. Known for their role in the Christiana Riot of 1851, in which they prevented the return of several fugitives to Maryland, Parker's band also was very active in the fight against kidnapping.[40] Parker shared a similar background with Frederick Douglass. Both men had escaped from slavery in Maryland and had dedicated their lives to helping other blacks and promoting abolitionism. They also shared the same attitude toward kidnapping and slave catching. As Parker put it, "Whether the kidnappers were clothed with legal authority or not, I did not care to inquire, as I never had faith in nor respect for the Fugitive-Slave Law."[41]

As a young man, William Parker had escaped from Maryland and settled just across the state line in southeastern Pennsylvania. He reported that true freedom did not come with his escape to a free state. "After a few years of life in a Free State, the enthusiasm of the lad materially sobered down," Parker recounted, "and I found, by bitter experience, that to preserve my stolen liberty I must pay, unremittingly, an almost sleepless vigilance." Kidnapping in this region was so common, Parker related, that blacks there lived in continual fear. Every two or three weeks, slave catchers or kidnappers attempted to capture someone.[42] Blacks in the area were particularly provoked by a ring of slave catchers and kidnappers known as the Gap Gang, described as a "loosely organized band of working-class whites who terrorized the Black community of Lancaster County."[43] After several people had been abducted by the gang, "the anti-slavery friends and the colored people in Sadbury township became more vigilant, meeting frequently and taking counsel with each other." Strangers who came into the region were carefully watched and blacks were warned of any suspicious behavior.[44] From the actions of even the legal slave catchers, it appears that Parker and his friends were justified in making no distinction between them and kidnappers. Such persons often broke into a home, beat the inhabitants, and carried their victims off at gunpoint. As a result, Parker and others "formed an organization for mutual protection against slaveholders and kidnappers."[45]

The resolve of the group is illustrated by one of the numerous incidents described by Parker. A black girl who lived at the home of Moses Whitson, an abolitionist from a neighboring county, was seized by three men. Although they claimed she was their slave, the girl denied knowing any of them. They tied her up and drove toward the state line. A neighbor, Benjamin Whipper, sounded the alarm, and Parker and several others gave chase. They overtook the kidnappers, released the captive, and then beat the kidnappers so severely that two died. Parker recounted several similar incidents; in some of these his band triumphed, in others they did not. In most cases, it is unclear whether or not the people abducted were actually free blacks or runaway slaves. But the behavior of the slave catchers gave no clue, for they apparently did not follow the law in recovering their property. Instead, they simply arrived armed and forcibly took whom they wanted. The activities of Parker and his gang show the degree to which blacks, those legally free and those who had freed themselves, defended each other, even at the risk of their own lives.[46]

Blacks organized for self-defense particularly in reaction to the indiscriminate actions of slave catchers and kidnappers after the Fugitive Slave Law of 1850 was enacted and given extensive publicity by abolitionists. Many blacks fled to Canada in fear of the law, but the majority did not.[47] Both fugitives and free blacks throughout the free states armed themselves, reported abolitionist Henry C. Wright. "It is said that one store in Pittsburg [sic] sold, in one day, last week, over thirty revolvers—from four to six barrels each—and twice as many bowie knives, to the colored people and their friends."[48]

Blacks also took the opportunity while defending themselves against kidnappers and slave catchers to educate whites about the dangers that blacks faced. Charles H. Langston went on trial for breaking the Fugitive Slave Law of 1850 through his involvement in the famous Oberlin-Wellington rescue in 1858. Langston, brother of postbellum Virginia Congressman John Mercer Langston, got his chance when the judge asked why he should not be sentenced. The defendant attacked the law, stating, "Some may say that there is no danger of free persons being seized and carried off as slaves. No one need labor under such a delusion." Several people taken under the 1850 Fugitive Slave Law had been enslaved even after proving their free status, Langston noted. His speech so moved the court that he was given a lesser sentence than his white accomplice.[49]

Historians have provided us with an increasingly detailed picture of free black life prior to the Civil War. The majority faced disenfranchisement, social ostracization, and extreme poverty. Free blacks were not free in the way that whites were. They often met not merely prejudice from American whites, but violence as well. Kidnapping was one example of their vulnerability. People of color could be easily enslaved, legally or illegally, as they lived in a legal limbo between slavery and freedom. Their freedom was greatly compromised by various restrictions, and they could be robbed of it at any time.

Free blacks, however, did not suffer in silence. They battled the crime of kidnapping at all levels of government, consistently reminding white officials of their humanity and their rights. They addressed the problem both on a case-by-case basis and through the formation of organizations designed to aid free blacks who were illegally enslaved. And when legal methods failed them, free blacks took the law into their own hands and protected themselves. Each tactic represented a great risk to free black protesters. They faced white apathy, even hostility; the most extreme risks were being kidnapped, even killed. But leaders such as Richard Allen, David Ruggles, and William Parker and their followers were prepared to risk all to preserve their grip on freedom.

Conclusion

After a kidnapping occurred in Philadelphia, Quaker educator Anthony Benezet asked, "Alas! how many, both of parents and children, may be taken from their free homes into bondage, terminating only with life." [1] As Winfield Collins noted of the *Liberator's* attempt to quantify kidnapping, the number of incidents that were discovered and recorded was probably substantially lower than the number of kidnappings that actually occurred. [2] Assuming that this judgment is correct, it is likely that kidnapping produced great fear within the black community. The New York Vigilance Committee reported in 1837 that the kidnapping of free blacks had become so extensive that no free black person was safe. [3] And that is the crucial issue. Not every free black was kidnapped, nor did every free black know someone who had been. But judging by the number of individual cases and the response to kidnapping, it appears that most blacks must have known about the dreaded possibility of abduction into slavery. The fact that kidnapping could occur, even to such upstanding citizens as Richard Allen and David Ruggles, was enough to make the free black population, especially those making their homes near slave states, live in perpetual fear.

This constant dread of losing their freedom fundamentally distinguished the experience of free blacks from that of whites. Historians have noted many distinctions between freedom for blacks and whites, but for blacks, even the conditions of daily life were often closer to slavery than freedom. Because of the restrictions on the free black population, by law and by custom, free blacks did not enjoy the same liberty that whites did. Even the term "free black" is really a misnomer, as Ira Berlin noted when he called free blacks "slaves without masters."[4]

Nevertheless, free blacks were not legally slaves. Free blacks might have suffered under numerous burdens, economic, political, and social, but they still enjoyed the legal distinction, if only on paper, of not being owned by another human being. They were people, not property. The prevalence of kidnapping, however, demonstrates that free blacks could rapidly and easily become property. Just as slaves became free by way of the Underground Railroad, so did free people become slaves by what Julie Winch has termed "the other Underground Railroad."[5] And once free blacks were enslaved, it was likely that they would remain so.

Bill G. Smith and Richard Wojtowicz discovered *Pennsylvania Gazette* advertisements in the colonial period for fugitives who claimed to be free. They surmised that before the Revolution, "many blacks without masters may have led the lives of fugitives, real and imagined"[6] Free black status, then, was compromised not only by various restrictions that limited the exercise of citizenship, but also by a tenuous quality that was not characteristic of white freedom. Because free blacks could become slaves so readily, the very concept of black freedom was of a truly precarious nature. "Where a traffic in slaves is thus actively carried on and sanctioned by exisiting laws," reported an 1827 edition of the *African Observer,* "those coloured persons who are legally free, must necessarily hold their freedom by a very precarious tenure, particularly where every person tinged with an African die [*sic*], is presumed to be a slave, unless proven to be free."[7]

The issue of kidnapping illuminates not only the lives of free blacks but also the mindset of the country as a whole. Historians have long puzzled over the question of how the United States, a nation founded on the basis of freedom and democracy, began as a slave society. Edmund Morgan has hypothesized that it was the very existence of slavery that freed the country's leaders from the threat of class warfare and allowed them to devote their time and energies to founding and running the country. Slavery stabilized the new nation by uniting whites at a crucial time. It was also necessary to safeguard the newfound freedom, it was believed, by not extending it to those deemed incapable of defending it. Black slavery, therefore, helped secure white freedom during the Revolution.[8]

The existence of a class of free blacks, however, revealed a gray area between slavery and freedom. Revolutionary leaders were not oblivious to the discrepancy of a slave state's fighting for its own freedom from another country. To some extent, the commonly held belief in black inferiority lessened the paradox. But the survival of slavery continued to discomfort many, including slaveowners like Thomas Jefferson. Ambivalence over the system of slavery was prevalent in the early days of the Republic; the defense of slavery as "a positive good" belonged to a later generation. The ambivalence over the right of individuals to own other individuals, and the deleterious effect on the slaves' humanity, may have been reflected by whites' grudging acceptance of a free black class. It is possible that allowing a certain segment of the slave population to gain freedom was a way of assuaging white guilt over slavery. That whites never felt comfortable with the existence of free blacks is made clear by the numerous forms of control, legal and illegal, under which free blacks lived. In addition to the legal methods of control, such as disenfranchisement and restriction of movement, free blacks also were forced to abide by customs that prevented them from living in certain areas and working at certain jobs. More frightening forms of extralegal control existed as well when racism manifested itself in violence. This was supported by a legal system that found crimes against black persons to be negligible and, when committed by whites, virtually unprosecutable.

As such, kidnapping may have served a function in antebellum America analogous to that of lynching following the Civil War. There are many similarities between the two crimes. Violence was often present in kidnapping, always so in lynching. Lynching resulted in the termination of an individual's life, while kidnapping brought what might have seemed like a slow death to someone previously free. Both practices reflected a disrespect for legal safeguards, including inaction on the part of public officials. Both provided benefits to whites, at the very least maintenance of the racist status quo. And both had a long history in the United States. Ultimately, both of these black marks on America's race relations record occurred because white Americans condoned these evils. As Robert L. Zangrando describes it in his study of lynching, "A gruesome instrument of social control, lynching exposed white America's contempt for black people and its disregard for duly constituted legal procedures."[9] Kidnapping can be described in the same manner.

Was the tacit acceptance of kidnapping by the majority of the white population another method of control, a further reflection of the fact that while the idea of slavery may have caused whites some discomfort, the free black population caused even more? The toleration of kidnapping was a way for whites to enslave free blacks without admitting that they were doing so. At the same time, the ever-present threat of kidnapping provided a constant reminder to free blacks that even though they were not slaves, they were nevertheless black, and the autonomy they possessed could be stolen from them at any moment.

Notes

Introduction

1. Ira Berlin, *Slaves Without Masters: The Free Negro in the Antebellum South* (New York: Pantheon Books, 1974). For a detailed discussion of discrimination against free blacks, see Berlin; Leon F. Litwack, *North of Slavery: The Negro in the Free States* (Chicago: Univ. of Chicago Press, 1961).

2. T.H. Breen and Stephen Innes, *Myne Owne Ground: Race and Freedom on Virginia's Eastern Shore, 1640-1676* (New York: Oxford Univ. Press, 1980). See also Oscar and Mary F. Handlin, "Origins of the Southern Labor System," *William and Mary Quarterly*, series 3, 7 (April 1950): 199-222.

3. Winthrop Jordan, *White Over Black: American Attitudes Toward the Negro, 1550-1812* (Chapel Hill: Univ. of North Carolina Press, 1968), 3-25; Carl N. Degler, "Slavery and the Genesis of American Race Prejudice," *Comparative Studies in Society and History* 2 (Oct. 1959): 49-66; Edmund S. Morgan, *American Slavery, American Freedom: The Ordeal of Colonial Virginia* (New York: W.W. Norton, 1975).

4. Philip D. Curtin, *The Atlantic Slave Trade: A Census* (Madison: Univ. of Wisconsin Press, 1969), 268. For a detailed account of the kidnapping of Africans into slavery in the Americas, see Curtin; John W. Blassingame, *The Slave Community: Plantation Life in the Antebellum South* (New York: Oxford Univ. Press, 1979); Carl N. Degler, *Neither Black Nor White: Slavery and Race Relations in Brazil and the United States* (New York: Macmillan, 1971).

5. Robert Louis Stevenson, *Kidnapped* (New York: Charles Scribner's Sons, 1905); quote from James Fulton Zimmerman, *Impressment of American Seamen* (New York: Columbia Univ. Press, 1925), 12.

6. Morgan, *American Slavery, American Freedom*, 32-33; Abbot Emerson Smith, *Colonists in Bondage: White Servitude and Convict*

Labor in America, 1607-1776 (Chapel Hill: Univ. of North Carolina Press, 1947), 67-70.

7. Eric Williams, "Slavery in the West Indies," in *Slavery: A Comparative Perspective*, ed. Robin W. Winks (New York: New York Univ. Press, 1972), 28.

8. Peter Wilson Coldham, "The 'Spiriting' of London Children to Virginia, 1648-1685," *Virginia Magazine of History and Biography* 83 (July 1975): 280; Robert C. Johnson, "The Transportation of Vagrant Children from London to Virginia, 1618-1622," in *Early Stuart Studies*, ed. H.S. Reinmuth, Jr. (Minneapolis: Univ. of Minnesota Press, 1970), 137-38.

9. Liberator, 25 Oct. 1850.

10. Ibid., 27 April 1833.

11. Ibid.

12. Ibid., 26 Feb. 1831 (from the *New Orleans Mercantile Advertiser*).

13. Nevertheless, the stealing of slaves occurred. Abram Harris, for example, who was born a slave near Greenville, South Carolina, recalled that he and his sister Delia had been stolen when they were about twelve or thirteen years old. Their abductors came in the night, seized the two children, and hid them in the woods. Abram and his sister were then yoked together with a group of several other children, and made to walk to Georgia, where they were sold. Norman Yetman, ed., *Voices From Slavery* (New York: Holt and Rinehart, 1970), 159-160. Likewise, a man was arrested in Girard, Alabama, for abducting "Abe," the slave of P.B. Brown. "Abe," described as "a mulatto, fine-looking, and very intelligent," had been hired out as a ticket collector at the railroad depot in Macon. Because of his job, "Abe" may have been mistaken for a free black. Columbus, *Daily Sun* (Georgia), 9 July 1856. Henry Lewis, born on a Pine Island, Georgia, plantation, provided more evidence of slave stealing. He remembered that slave traders came through the area, fixing camp on the edge of town. "Old Massa warn us look out and not let de trader cotch us, 'cause a trader just as soon as steal a nigger and sell him." While Lewis's master probably overrated the danger of slave stealing, the practice certainly occurred. Yetman, *Voices*, 106.

14. For more information on fugitive slaves, see Stanley Campbell, *The Slave-Catchers: Enforcement of the Fugitive Slave Law, 1850-1860* (Chapel Hill: Univ. of North Carolina Press, 1970); Mar-

ion Gleason McDougall, *Fugitive Slaves, 1619-1865* (Boston: Ginn and Company, 1891).

15. U.B. Phillips, *American Negro Slavery* (1918; Baton Rouge: Louisiana State University Press, 1966), 443.

16. Northup, Solomon, *Twelve Years a Slave* (London: Miller, Orton, and Mulligan, 1854), 252.

17. John Parrish, *Remarks on the Slavery of Black People* (Philadelphia: Kimber and Conrad, 1806), 9.

18. Kidnapping may have occurred during the colonial period as well, but to prevent the study from becoming too cumbersome, I have chosen to examine kidnapping only after the Revolution. For examples, see advertisements for fugitive slaves, a number of whom claimed to be free, in Billy G. Smith and Richard Wojtowicz, "The Precarious Freedom of Blacks in the Mid–Atlantic Region: Excerpts from the *Pennsylvania Gazette*, 1728-1776," *Pennsylvania Magazine of History and Biography* 113 (April 1989): 237.

19. Eliza Cope Harrison, ed., *Philadelphia Merchant: The Diary of Thomas P. Cope, 1800-1851* (South Bend, Ind.: Gateway Editions, 1978), 137.

1. "From Their Free Homes into Bondage": The Abduction of Free Blacks into Slavery

1. *Courier and Enquirer* (New Hampshire), 25 Nov. 1836.

2. Yetman, *Voices*, 121.

3. Levi Coffin, *Reminiscences of Levi Coffin* (1876; New York: Arno Press, 1968), 12.

4. Jesse Torrey, *A Portraiture of Domestic Slavery in the United States*, 2d ed. (Ballston Spa, N.Y.: Privately published, 1818), 95.

5. U.S. Bureau of the Census, *Negro Population in the United States, 1790-1915* (Washington, D.C.: Government Printing Office, 1918), 57.

6. William M. Wiecek, *The Sources of Antislavery: Constitutionalism in America, 1760-1848* (Ithaca: Cornell Univ. Press, 1977), 88.

7. *National Anti-Slavery Standard*, 14 Nov. 1857.

8. *Cincinnati Gazette*, 25 July 1857.

9. Northup, *Twelve Years a Slave*, 3, 9, 12-20, 48, 61, 212-214, 225-228, 242, 243-251, 256-266. *New York Times*, 20 Jan. 1854.

10. *Cleveland Leader*, 10 July 1854.

11. Torrey, *Portraiture of Slavery*, 81-83; deposition of Jesse Torrey, 29 April 1816, in Papers of the Select Committee to Inquire into the Existence of an Inhuman and Illegal Traffic in Slaves . . . in the District of Columbia, National Archives.

12. Torrey, *Portraiture of Slavery*, 97.

13. George Murray McConnel, "Illinois and Its People," *Transactions of the Illinois Historical Society*, no. 7 (Springfield, Ill., 1902), 80-81.

14. Ibid., 81-82.

15. Ibid.

16. Berlin, *Slaves Without Masters*, 226.

17. *National Anti-Slavery Standard*, 3 April 1858, 29 Jan. 1859; *Niles National Register*, 24 March 1858.

18. Kate E.R. Pickard, *The Kidnapped and Ransomed* (1856; New York: Negro Universities Press, 1968).

19. *National Anti-Slavery Standard*, 7 Nov. 1844.

20. *Montreal Gazette*, 31 Jan. 1861.

21. *Liberator*, 27 March 1863 (from the *Dedham [Massachusetts] Gazette*); Paul M. Angle and Earl Schenck Miers, *Tragic Years, 1860-1865* (New York: Simon and Schuster, 1960), 2:463.

22. Otto Eisenschiml and Ralph Newman, *The American Iliad* (Lexington: Univ. of Kentucky Press,), 136; Edwin B. Coddington, *The Gettysburg Campaign: A Study in Command* (New York: Charles Scribner's Sons, 1968), 150, 161.

23. *Liberator*, 27 March 1863 (from *Correspondence of the Fond du Lac (Wisconsin) Commonwealth*); Reid Mitchell, *Civil War Soldiers* (New York: Viking, 1988), 123.

24. Delaware Abolition Society (hereafter DAS), Minutes, 4 Jan. 1816, Historical Society of Pennsylvania (hereafter HSP).

25. Kenneth M. Stampp, *The Peculiar Institution: Slavery in the Ante-Bellum South* (New York: Vintage Books, 1956), 415-16.

26. Gary B. Nash, "Forging Freedom: The Emancipation Experience in the Northern Seaport Cities, 1775-1820," in Ira Berlin and Ronald Hoffman, eds., *Slavery and Freedom in the Age of the American Revolution*, (Charlottesville: Univ. of Virginia Press, 1983), 11.

27. *African Observer*, July 1827.

28. DAS Minutes, 4 Jan. 1816, HSP.

29. Edward Needles, *An Historical Memoir of the Pennsylvania Society for Promoting the Abolition of Slavery* (1848; New York: Arno Press and New York Times, 1969), 62.

30. Bureau of the Census, *Negro Population*, 55.

31. Minutes of the American Convention, 1828, in "Reports of the American Convention of Abolition Societies on Negroes and Slavery, Their Appeals to Congress, and Their Addresses to the Citizens of the United States," *Journal of Negro History* 6 (July 1921): 327.

32. *Frankfort Yeoman*, 18 Nov. 1854.

33. Dwight L. Dumond, ed., *Letters of James Gillespie Birney* (1938; Gloucester, Mass.: Peter Smith, 1966), 2:652.

34. Pennsylvania Abolition Society (hereafter PAS), Acting Committee Minutes, 30 Nov. 1819, HSP.

35. Ibid.

36. Ibid.

37. Ibid.

38. Ibid.

39. James Rogers to Joseph Watson, 14 Feb. 1826, in "Negroes Kidnapped" (hereafter NK), Delaware Hall of Records (hereafter DHR).

40. George Alfred Townshend, *The Entailed Hat* (1884; Cambridge, Md.: Tidewater Publishing, 1955); R.W. Messenger, *Patty Cannon Administers Justice, or Joe Johnson's Last Kidnapping Exploit* (1926; Cambridge, Md.: Tidewater Publishing, 1960); Ted Giles, *Patty Cannon: Woman of Mystery* (Easton, Md.: Easton Publishing, 1965); *Narrative and Confessions of Lucretia P. Cannon* (New York: 1841).

41. *Narrative and Confessions*, 10.

42. PAS, Acting Committee Minutes, vol. 4 (1810-22), pp. 72-74 (letter of John Kollock to the PAS, 26 August 1815), HSP; "Alleged Runaway Slaves—Various Cases Stated—Decision of the Magistrates and of the Supreme Court of Pennsylvania, Received from Friends, 13 January 1817," in Papers of the Select Committee on the African Slave Trade, National Archives (hereafter NA).

43. PAS, Acting Committee Minutes, 1 Jan. 1816, 12 June 1816, 16 Oct. 1816, HSP; "Alleged Runaway Slaves," in Papers of the Select Committee on the African Slave Trade, NA.

44. PAS, Acting Committee Minutes, vol. 4, pp. 130, 139; HSP.

45. Deposition of Judge Cranch, 7 March 1816, Circuit Court, City of Washington, D.C., petition for freedom of John Parker and Rosanna Brown, Isaac Gibbs for John Reynolds to B.L. Lear, 5 Jan. 1816, in Papers of the Select Committee on Illegal Traffic in Slaves in the District, NA.

46. John Henderson to Joseph Watson, 2 Jan. 1826, Joseph Watson Papers (hereafter JWP), HSP; *African Observer*, May 1827.

47. *African Observer*, May 1827.

48. Ibid.

49. Ibid.

50. James Rogers to Joseph Watson, 14 Feb. 1826, NK, DHR.

51. Thomas Garrett to Joseph Watson, 20 Feb. 1826; Ebenezer Blackston to Joseph Watson, 10 March 1826, JWP, HSP.

52. Jesse Green to Joseph Watson, 28 Feb. 1826, JWP, HSP.

53. James Bryan to Joseph Watson, 18 March 1826, JWP, HSP.

54. Thomas Layton to James Rogers, 26 Feb. 1826, JWP, HSP.

55. Joseph Watson to Spencer Francis, 20 March 1826, NK, DHR.

56. Richard Stockton to Joseph Watson, 26 May 1826, in *African Observer*, May 1827, pp. 41–42.

57. Narrative of Samuel Scomp, 30 June 1826, in *African Observer*, May 1827.

58. Ibid.

59. Ibid.

60. Joseph Watson to William Rawle, 4 July 1826, PAS Correspondence, Incoming, 1826, HSP.

61. Both Joseph E. Davis and Duncan S. Walker were the brothers of more famous men. Davis's brother was Jefferson Davis, eventually president of the Confederacy. Walker's brother was Robert J. Walker, who served as governor of the Kansas Territory and as President James Polk's Secretary of the Treasury. The Walkers, Holmes, and Henderson all were originally from the Mid-Atlantic (New Jersey and Pennsylvania), which may help explain why a group of Mississippians were willing to help the kidnapping victims in this case.

62. David Holmes and J.E. Davis to Joseph Watson, 23 Dec. 1826, in *African Observer*, May 1827, p. 43; narrative of Peter Hook, ibid.

63. Narrative of Peter Hook.

64. Joseph Watson to David Holmes and J.E. Davis, 20 Jan. 1826, in *African Observer*, May 1827.

65. Joseph Watson to Duncan S. Walker, 24 Jan. 1827, ibid.

66. "In Select Council," 8 Feb. 1827, JWP.

67. Proclamation, 9 Feb. 1827, in *African Observer*, May 1827, pp. 44–45.

68. Joseph Watson to Duncan S. Walker, 24 Jan. 1827, ibid., pp. 45–46.

69. Duncan S. Walker to Joseph Watson, 25 Feb. 1827, ibid., pp. 46-47.

70. Narrative of Lydia Smith, ibid.

71. Joseph Watson to James Rogers, 24 Feb. 1827, NK, DHR.

72. Joseph Watson to John Hamilton, 24 Feb. 1827, JWP, HSP.

73. Joseph Watson to John Hamilton and John Henderson, 10 March 1829, JWP, HSP.

74. Jesse Green to Joseph Watson, 12 March 1827, JWP, HSP.

75. *African Observer*, May 1827.

76. Joshua Boucher to Joseph Watson, 17 Jan. 1827, JWP, HSP.

77. Ibid., 23 March 1827, JWP, HSP.

78. Thomas Garrett to Joseph Watson, 3 May 1827, JWP, HSP.

79. Newspaper clipping, 7 May 1827, JWP, HSP.

80. Quarter Sessions, Court of General Sessions, Sussex County Docket, 1820-26, DHR.

81. Ibid.

82. *Delaware Gazette and American Watchman*, 10 April 1829.

83. Ibid.

84. Ibid., 10 and 17 April 1829.

85. Quarter Sessions, Court of General Sessions, Sussex County Docket, 1826-37, DHR.

86. *Narrative and Confessions*, 16.

87. Quarter Sessons, Court of General Sessions, Sussex County Docket, 1826-37, DHR.

88. Court of Oyer and Terminer Docket, Sussex County, 1823-29, DHR.

89. *Narrative and Confessions*, 22-23.

90. Quarter Sessions, Court of General Sessions, Sussex County Docket, 1820-26, DHR.

91. *African Observer*, August 1827.

92. "Kidnapping," undated newspaper clipping, JWP, HSP.

93. Ibid.

94. Ibid.

95. *African Observer*, August 1827.

96. *Niles National Register*, 23 June 1827.

97. Ibid., 10 April 1824.

98. *Delaware Gazette and American Watchman*, 19 May 1829.

99. *Baltimore Sun*, 3 April 1955.

100. Ibid. and 31 March 1907. Today the town of Reliance stands at the site of the Cannon-Johnson homes. Formerly called John-

son's Crossroads, the town was renamed in 1882 because of the negative connotation.

101. *Baltimore Sun*, 31 March 1907.

102. Ibid., 3 April 1955.

103. Samuel S. May, *The Fugitive Slave Law and Its Victims*, rev. ed. (New York: American Anti-Slavery Society, 1861), 154.

104. PAS Acting Committee Minutes, vol. 5 1822–42), p. 43, HSP.

105. *Albany Evening Journal*, 1 Dec. 1857, from the *Cincinnati Commercial*.

106. Statement of Isaiah Sadler, 13 Sept. 1824, JWP, HSP.

2. "The Legitimate Offspring of Slavery": Kidnappers Who Operated within the Law

1. Berlin, *Slaves Without Masters*, 182–184, 188–190.

2. George M. Stroud, *A Sketch of the Laws Relating to Slavery in the Several States of the United States of America*, 2d ed. (Philadelphia: Henry Longstreth, 1856), 272–73.

3. Campbell, *Slave-Catchers*, 10.

4. Don E. Fehrenbacher, *The Dred Scott Case: Its Significance in American Law and Politics* (New York: Oxford Univ. Press, 1978), 21; Wilbur H. Seibert, *The Underground Railroad From Slavery to Freedom* (1898; New York: Russell and Russell, 1967), 295; Harold M. Hyman and William M. Wiecek, *Equal Justice Under the Law: Constitutional Development, 1835-1875* (New York: Harper and Row, 1982), 105.

5. Hyman and Wiecek, *Equal Justice*, 149.

6. Stroud, *Laws Relating to Slavery*, 273; Philip S. Foner, *History of Black Americans*, vol. 3, *From the Compromise of 1850 to the End of the Civil War* (Westport, Conn.: Greenwood Press, 1983), 9.

7. Stroud, *Laws Relating to Slavery*, 279–80; Campbell, *Slave-Catchers*, 24.

8. Campbell, *Slave-Catchers*, 24.

9. David Potter, *The Impending Crisis, 1848-1861* (New York: Harper and Row, 1976), 131.

10. *North American and United States Gazette* (Philadelphia), 30 July 1860.

11. *Liberator*, 15 Jan. 1831.

12. Monongalia County Court Records 1837, West Virginia

Collection (hereafter wvc), West Virginia University (hereafter wvu).

13. William G. Hawkins, *Lunsford Lane; or, Another Helper from North Carolina* (1863; New York: Negro Universities Press, 1969), 103–8.

14. Hawkins, *Lunsford Lane*, 109–12.

15. Lunsford Lane, *The Narrative of Lunsford Lane* (Boston: Privately printed, 1842); *Anti-Slavery Reporter*, 27 July 1842.

16. *Lawrence (Kansas) Republican*, 4 Aug. 1860.

17. May, *The Fugitive Slave Law*, 137–38.

18. Peter C. Ripley and Jeffrey S. Rossbach, eds., *The Black Abolitionist Papers*, vol. 1, *British Isles, 1830-1865* (Chapel Hill: Univ. of North Carolina Press, 1985), 195.

19. *Voice of the Fugitive*, 6 May 1852.

20. For more about the use of the states' rights argument by antislavery people, see Paul Finkelman, "Prigg v. Pennsylvania and Northern State Courts: Anti-slavery Use of a Pro-Slavery Decision," *Civil War History* 25 (March 1979): 25.

21. Paul Finkelman, "Slavery and the Constitutional Convention: Making a Convenant with Death," in Richard Beeman, Stephen Botein, and Edward C. Carter III, eds., *Beyond Confederation: Origins of the Constitution and American National Identity* (Chapel Hill: Univ. of North Carolina Press, 1987), 190–191, 223; William M. Wiecek, *The Sources of Anti-Slavery Constitutionalism in America, 1760-1848* (Ithaca: Cornell Univ. Press, 1977), 62–63.

22. Max Farrand, ed., *The Records of the Federal Convention of 1787* (New Haven: Yale Univ. Press, 1911) 2:369–79, 443, 449–53.

23. U.S. Constitution, Article 1, sections 8 and 9; Article 4, section 2.

24. Finkelman, "Slavery and the Constitutional Convention," 224; David Brion Davis, *The Problem of Slavery in the Age of the Revolution, 1770-1823* (Ithaca: Cornell Univ. Press, 1975), 130–31.

25. Staughton Lynd, *Class Conflict, Slavery, and the United States Constitution* (New York: Bobbs–Merrill, 1967), 159.

26. Walter M. Merrill, *Against Wind and Tide: A Biography of William Lloyd Garrison* (Cambridge: Harvard Univ. Press, 1963), 204; Weicek, *Sources of Anti-Slavery*, 228–48; Lynd, *Class Conflict*, 154–55.

27. Eric Foner, *Free Soil, Free Labor, Free Men: The Ideology of the Republican Party before the Civil War* (New York: Oxford Univ.

Press, 1970), 73, 76, 84, 89; Wiecek, *Sources of Anti-Slavery*, 208–27; Lynd, *Class Conflict*, 154.

28. PAS Minutes, Memorial to Governor Mifflin, vol. 1 (1775–1800), pp. 154–56, HSP; *Pennsylvania Archives*, series 4, vol. 4, Governor Mifflin's speech to the Pennsylvania legislature, 24 Aug. 1791; *American State Papers*, Class X, Misc. vol 1 (Washington, D.C.: Gales and Seaton, 1834), 38–43.

29. Seibert, *The Underground Railroad*, 295.

30. *United States Statutes*, vol. 1 1st–5th Congresses (1789–1799) (Boston: Little, Brown, and Company, 1845), 302–05. For a more detailed account of the development of the 1793 fugitive slave law, see Paul Finkelman, "The Kidnapping of John Davis and the Adoption of the Fugitive Slave Law of 1793," *Journal of Southern History* 56 (Aug. 1990): 397–422. See also William R. Leslie, "A Study in the Origins of Interstate Rendition: The Big Beaver Creek Murders," *American Historical Review* 57 (October 1951): 63–75, which views the 1793 law as a result of conflict over the murder of four Pennsylvania Indians by several Virginia men.

31. Testimony of Andrew Ellicott before the Select Committee on the African Slave Trade, NA.

32. *Liberator*, 7 June 1834.

33. Torrey, *Portraiture of Slavery*, 97.

34. John C. Hurd, *The Laws of Freedom and Bondage in the United States*, vol. 2 (Boston: Little, Brown, 1858–59), 72.

35. Peter A. Browne, *A Review of the Trial, Conviction, and Sentence of George F. Alberti, for Kidnapping* (Philadelphia: 1851), 2–3; *Commonwealth of Pennsylvania v. James Frisby Price, George F. Alberti, and J.G. Mitchell*, Court of Oyer and Terminer and Quarter Sessions, City and County of Philadelphia, Dec. 1850, City Hall, Philadelphia.

36. Browne, "A Review of the Trial," 3, 4, 7.

37. *National Anti-Slavery Standard*, 19 Feb. 1859.

38. Browne, "A Review of the Trial," 7.

39. Paul Finkelman, *Slavery in the Courtroom: An Annotated Bibliography of American Cases* (Washington, D.C.: Library of Congress, 1985), 83–85.

40. PAS Acting Committee Minutes, 21 Dec. 1815, 19 May 1818, HSP.

41. PAS Acting Committee Minutes, 21 March 1839, HSP.

42. *Liberator*, 17 Nov. 1837.

43. *Commonwealth of Pennsylvania v. George F. Alberti, J. Frisby*

Price, Robert Smith, George T. Price, John Diggin, William McKinley, Court of Oyer and Terminer and Quarter Sessions, City and County of Philadelphia, February 1851, City Hall, Philadelphia; *Pennsylvania Freeman* 20 (26 Dec. 1850); Thomas J. Scharf and Thompson Westcott, *History of Philadelphia, 1609-1884* (Philadelphia: L.H. Everts, 1884), 1:701; and May, *The Fugitive Slave Law,* 12.

44. Ibid.

45. *National Anti-Slavery Standard,* 19 Feb. 1859.

46. Finkelman, "Prigg v. Pennsylvania," 34; Campbell, *The Slave-Catchers,* 9; Foner, *History of Black Americans* 3:5.

47. *United States Statutes,* vol. 9, 1845-1851 (Boston: Little, Brown, 1851), 462-65 (21st Cong., 1st sess.).

48. Stroud, *A Sketch of the Laws Relating to Slavery,* 273.

49. Ibid, 280; *Pennsylvania Freeman,* 26 Dec. 1850.

50. Campbell, *The Slave-Catchers,* 41.

51. John G. Palfrey, "Letter to a Whig Neighbor, on the Approaching State Election, by an Old Conservative" (Boston: Crosby, Nichols, 1855), 10.

52. Wendell Phillips, "Argument of Wendell Phillips, Esq. against the Repeal of the Personal Liberty Law, before the Committee of the Legislature, Tuesday, January 29, 1861" (Boston: R.F. Wallcutt, 1861) in *Anti-Slavery Tracts,* series 2 (nos. 15-25), 1861 (Westport, Conn.: Negro Universities Press, 1970), 4.

53. Stroud, *Laws Relating to Slavery,* 280.

54. Scharf and Westcott, *History of Philadelphia* 1:701.

55. *Philadelphia Daily News, Daily Sun, Spirit of the Times,* quoted in *Pennsylvania Freeman,* 20 Dec. 1850.

56. Hyman and Wiecek, *Equal Justice,* 149.

57. N. Dwight Harris, *The History of Negro Servitude in Illinois, 1719-1864* (1904; New York: Negro Universities Press, 1969), 56-57.

58. J. Winston Coleman, *Slavery Times in Kentucky* (Chapel Hill: Univ. of North Carolina Press, 1940), 206-7.

59. Edward Raymond Turner, *The Negro in Pennsylvania: Slavery, Servitude, Freedom, 1739-1861* (1911; New York: Negro Universities Press, 1969), 242.

60. David Potter, *The Impending Crisis, 1848-1861* (New York: Harper and Row, 1976), 131.

61. Berlin, *Slaves Without Masters,* 138.

62. Hurd, *Laws of Freedom and Bondage* 1:90-97, 151, 191.

63. Foner, *History of Black Americans,* vol. 2: *From the Emergence*

of the Cotton Kingdom to the Eve of the Compromise of 1850, 164; Berlin, *Slaves Without Masters*, 138.

64. *Cincinnati Gazette*, 26, 27 Oct. 1857.

65. *Albany (New York) Evening Journal*, 27 April 1858; Hurd, *Laws of Freedom and Bondage* 1:3–4.

66. Hurd, *Laws of Freedom and Bondage* 1:136; Mary Frances Berry and John W. Blassingame, *Long Memory: The Black Experience in America* (New York: Oxford Univ. Press, 1982), 34; Ripley and Rossbach, *Black Abolitionist Papers* 1:374.

67. Lydia Maria Child, *An Appeal in Favor of that Class of Americans Called Africans* (Boston: Allen and Ticknor, 1833), 64; Hurd, *Laws of Freedom and Bondage* 1:9, 11.

68. Hurd, *Laws of Freedom and Bondage* 1:20, 97, 146.

69. Committee on the Judiciary Petitions—Protection of Free Colored Citizens within the Jurisdiction of the Several Slave States, 3–28 March 1854, NA.

70. Ira Dye, "Early American Merchant Seafarers," *Proceedings of the American Philosophical Society* 120 (1976): 331.

71. Gary B. Nash, "Forging Freedom," 8.

72. Dye, "Early American Merchant Seafarers," 333.

73. *Congressional Globe*, 31st Cong., 1st sess., appendix, part 2, 1677.

74. *National Anti-Slavery Standard*, 8 Oct. 1840.

75. Nash, "Forging Freedom," 8.

76. W. Jeffrey Bolster, "To Feel Like a Man: Black Seamen in the Northern States, 1800–1860," *Journal of American History* 76 (March 1990): 1174.

77. Acts of the State of South Carolina, 1822, Columbia, South Carolina, 1823, pp. 11–14.

78. Philip M. Hamer, "Great Britain, the United States, and the Negro Seamen Acts, 1822–1848," *Journal of Southern History* 1 (1935): 5. The practice of the time was for Supreme Court justices to spend some time presiding over lower federal courts.

79. Henry C. Wilson, *Rise and Fall of the Slave Power* (Boston: Houghton, Mifflin, 1872) 1:576; Hamer, "Negro Seamen Acts," 3–28.

80. *Voice of the Fugitive*, 6 May 1852.

81. Hamer, "Negro Seamen Acts", 3, 5, 18; Albert P. Blaustein and Robert L. Zangrando, eds., *Civil Rights and the Black American: A Documentary History*. 2d ed. (Chicago: Northwestern Univ. Press, 1991), 85–86.

82. *Anti-Slavery Advocate* (London), November 1853.

83. Hamer, "Negro Seamen Acts," 5-9, 22; *Congressional Globe*, 27th Cong. 3d sess., 384.

84. *Congressional Globe*, 27th Cong. 3d sess., 384.

85. "Samuel Hoar's Expulsion from Charleston," in *Old South Leaflets* no. 140 (Boston: Directors of the Old South Work, n.d.), 10-18; Hamer, "Negro Seamen Acts," 22. For a more detailed account of these incidents, see Wilson, *Rise and Fall of the Slave Power* 1:578-83.

86. Philip M. Hamer, "British Consuls and the Negro Seamen Acts, 1850-1860," *Journal of Southern History* 1 (1935): 168. For more on British relations with the South, see Laura A. White, "The South in the 1850's as seen by British Consuls," *Journal of Southern History* 1 (1935): 29-48.

87. *Congressional Globe*, 31st Cong., 1st sess., appendix, part 2, 1654-58. This congressional debate is also reprinted in part in both the *Liberator* 4, 11, 18, 25 October 1850, and *National Anti-Slavery Standard* 10, 25 Oct. 1850.

88. *Congressional Globe*, 31st Cong., 1st sess., appendix, part 2, 1674-78.

89. Bolster, "To Feel Like a Man," 1193; Lorenzo J. Greene, *The Negro in Colonial New England* (New York: Kennikat Press, 1966), 305.

90. Hurd, *Laws of Freedom and Bondage* 1:13, 21, 85, 195; Stroud, *Laws Relating to Slavery*, 28.

91. Hurd, *Laws of Freedom and Bondage* 1:92.

92. *National Intelligencer*, 3 March 1825.

93. *Woodville (Mississippi) Republican*, 19 Sept. 1835.

94. *Vicksburg (Alabama) Register*, 31 Dec. 1835.

95. Woodville (Mississippi) Republican 22 Dec. 1838.

96. Parrish, *Remarks on the Slavery of Black People*, 52, 53.

97. Monongalia County Court Records, box 22, envelope 114-A, wvc, wvu; Edward M. Steel, Jr., "Black Monongalians: A Judicial View of Slavery and the Negro in Monongalia County, 1776-1865," *West Virginia History* 34 (July 1973): 336.

98. *Liberator*, 11 May 1838.

99. *Leeds (England) Mercury*, 3 December 1853.

100. *Congressional Globe*, 28th Cong. 1st sess., 78; see also *National Anti-Slavery Standard*, 4 Jan. 1844.

101. *Congressional Debates*, 20th Cong. 2d sess., 67, 176-87, 191-92.

102. Senate Committee on the District of Columbia Folder, 6 Feb. to 10 Dec. 1844, NA; *Annals of Congress*, 28th Cong. 1st sess. 464–65, 678.

3. "Leave No Stone Unturned": Government Assistance to Free Blacks

1. *Liberator*, 7 June 1834.

2. Hurd, *The Laws of Freedom and Bondage*, 2, 5, 6, 29, 30, 34, 36, 37, 40, 42, 43, 48, 54, 66, 67, 70–74, 92, 106, 118, 127, 135, 136, 138, 140, 141, 146, 178.

3. Presentment of the Grand Jury of Baltimore, July 1816, in Papers of the Select Committee to Inquire into the Existence of an Inhuman and Illegal Traffic in Slaves . . . in the District of Columbia, NA.

4. Petitions on Negroes and Slavery, 1817, Delaware Legislative Papers, DHR.

5. *Delaware State Journal*, 8 Jan. 1839.

6. *Annals of Congress*, 4th Cong. 1st sess., 1025.

7. *Annals of Congress*, 4th Cong. 2d sess., 1730–37, 1895.

8. *Annals of Congress*, 14th Cong. 1st sess., 1115–17.

9. Deposition of Francis Scott Key, 22 April 1816; deposition of Judge Cranch, 7 March 1816; deposition of Jesse Torrey, 29 April 1816, in Papers of Select Committee to Inquire into the Existence of an Inhuman and Illegal Traffic in Slaves . . . in the District of Columbia, NA.

10. Papers of the Select Committee on the African Slave Trade, NA.

11. *Liberator*, 7 June 1834.

12. *Annals of Congress*, 14th Cong., 2d sess., 33, 36, 57–58, 65–66; 15 Cong., 1st sess., 61, 90, 92, 829; *United States Statutes*, May 21, 1866 (14 Stat. 50).

13. Finkelman, "Prigg v. Pennsylvania," 6; Thomas D. Morris, *Free Men All: The Personal Liberty Laws of the North 1780-1861* (Baltimore: Johns Hopkins Univ. Press, 1974), 94.

14. Morris, *Free Men All*, 45, 51–53.

15. Finkelman, "Prigg v. Pennsylvania," 7; Morris, *Free Men All*, 53, 94–95; Finkelman, *Slavery in the Courtroom*: 60–61.

16. Finkelman, "Prigg v. Pennsylvania," 7; Morris, *Free Men All*, 96–104; Finkelman, *Slavery in the Courtroom*, 61.

17. Morris, *Free Men All*, 104–6.

18. Finkelman, "Prigg v. Pennsylvania," 10; Jane H. Pease and William A. Pease, eds., *The Antislavery Argument* (New York: Bobbs-Merrill, 1965), lxxiv.

19. Pease and Pease, *Antislavery Argument*, lxxiv; Finkelman, "Prigg v. Pennsylvania," 10; Finkelman, *Slavery in the Courtroom*, 61.

20. Finkelman, "Prigg v. Pennsylvania," 22.

21. Hurd, *Laws of Freedom and Bondage* 1:32, 39, 121.

22. Campbell, *Slave-Catchers*, 27-28, 179-81; Morris, *Free Men All*, 168. For a list of all personal liberty and antikidnapping laws, see the appendix in Morris, *Free Men All*, 219-20.

23. *National Intelligencer*, 1 Aug. 1836.

24. Bayard Tuckerman, *William Jay and the Constitutional Movement for the Abolition of Slavery* (1893; New York: Franklin, 1969), 29-31; *Liberator*, 26 Oct. 1833.

25. Tuckerman, *William Jay*, 32-36.

26. Paul Finkelman, "The Protection of Black Rights in Seward's New York," *Civil War History* 53 (Sept. 1988): 212, 221.

27. Ibid., 213, 215; Starr Clark to William Seward, 15 April 1840 (copy), and Lewis Tappan to William Seward, 11 Jan. 1842 (copy), Seward Papers, University of Rochester.

28. *Albany Evening Journal*, 7 July 1860.

29. Finkelman, "Protection of Black Rights," 234.

30. Harris, *Negro Servitude in Illinois*, 32; E.B. Washburne, *Sketch of Edward Coles* (Chicago: Jansen, McClurg, 1882), 44, 65.

31. Douglas Polly's free papers (copy), bill of sale of the family (copy), depositions of John Rowe, H.M. Rust, John G. Medington, and Lorenzo D. Walton in *Martha Polly* v. *A.O. Robards*, in "Proofs and exhibits in the Peyton Polly case taken by J.W. Wilson, attorney for Ohio state and sent for executive files" (copy), Reuben Wood Papers (hereafter RWP), Ohio Historical Society (hereafter OHS).

32. Depositions of Jacob Heaberling and Colman Walker in *Peyton Polly* v. *John Watson* (copies), in Louisville Chancery Court Records (hereafter LCCR), Kentucky Department of Libraries and Archives (hereafter KDLA). This last file also contains the depositions of Rowe, Rust, Medington, and Walton, listed under *Peyton Polly* v. *John Watson*. The same file includes various documents such as bills, statement of complainant and amendments to that statement, decision of the court, which list the defendants variously as John Watson (later amended to Jerome), A.O. Hubbard

(apparently Robards), and Thomas Powell. Although all the documents refer to the same case, there was evidently some confusion over who was actually claiming ownership of the Pollys at any given time. Peyton Polly initially named Hubbard as the defendant in his statement to the court (dated 1 March 1851), and said that Hubbard intended to sell him immediately. Watson and/or Powell may have purchased one or more of the Pollys from Hubbard. An amendment to Polly's statement, dated the same day, however, explains that "he has had great difficulty in ascertaining who claimed him at the time of the institution of this suit. Ever since its institution he has been in jail and has been compelled to rely upon the information [of others]. He states that when he brought his suit he was in the possession of John Watson . . . and that Powell never had any interest in him." In another amendment, dated March 7, however, Polly claimed that the first statement (naming Hubbard as defendant) was prepared by his lawyer without his consultation. He claimed not to know Hubbard and stated that at the time of his being taken into custody he was held by Watson and Powell.

33. Depositions of Heaberling and Walker, LCCR, KDLA.

34. Records of the Appeals Court, State of Kentucky, in *Martha Polly* v. *A.O. Robards*, 30 June 1853, RWP, OHS; Memorandum-summary of the Peyton Polly case, 15 May 1856, Peyton Polly Papers (hereafter PPP), OHS.

35. Records of *Peyton Polly* v. *A.O. Robards*, 3 Oct. 1851, LCCR, KDLA (copy). Also in RWP, OHS.

36. Records of the Appeals Court, State of Kentucky, in *Louis Robards* v. *Martha*, 30 June 1853; James Harlan to Ralph Leete, 30 June 1853, RWP, OHS.

37. Ralph Leete to William Medill, 6 July 1853, RWP, OHS.

38. George B. Kinkead to Ralph Leete, 9 August 1853, Ralph Leete Papers (hereafter RLP), Western Reserve Historical Society (hereafter WRHS).

39. Memorandum—summary of the Peyton Polly case, 15 May 1856, PPP, OHS; payment to Ralph Leete, 10 Sept. 1851, RWP, WRHS.

40. Ralph Leete to Reuben Wood, 21 Oct. 1851, RWP, OHS.

41. Joel W. Wilson to Reuben Wood, August 1852, RWP, OHS.

42. George W. Summers to Ralph Leete, 30 Oct. 1851, RLP, WRHS. Summers's name is not clearly signed on the letter, but there are several indications that he is the author.

43. Joel W. Wilson to Reuben Wood, August 1852, RWP, OHS.

44. Joel W. Wilson to Salmon P. Chase, 27 Feb. 1856, Salmon P.

Chase Papers (hereafter SCP), OHS; Memorandum–summary of the Peyton Polly case, 15 May 1856, PPP, OHS; Ralph Leete to Salmon P. Chase, 25 July 1856, PPP, OHS.

45. Ralph Leete to Salmon P. Chase, 25 July 1856, PPP, OHS.

46. Salmon P. Chase to John Laidley, 18 March 1856, PPP, OHS.

47. John Laidley to Salmon P. Chase, 8 April 1857, PPP, OHS.

48. John Laidley to Salmon P. Chase, 15 Sept. 1857, PPP, OHS.

49. L.L. Rice to Salmon P. Chase, 16 Feb. 1859, PPP, OHS.

50. Records of the Circuit Court of Wayne County, Virginia, in *Pouley Paupers v. William Ratcliffe*, 22 March 1859, PPP, OHS.

51. A.M. Gangewer for Salmon P. Chase to Ralph Leete, 12 Nov. 1859, PPP, OHS.

52. Ralph Leete to A.M. Gangewer, 25 Nov. 1859, PPP, OHS.

53. William Dennison to Ralph Leete, 7 June 1860; Leete to Dennison, 16 June 1860, RLP, WRHS.

4. "The Thought of Slavery Is Death to a Free Man": Abolitionist Response to Kidnapping

1. Wiecek, *Sources of Antislavery*, 84; Silvio A. Bedini, *The Life of Benjamin Banneker* (New York: Charles Scribner's Sons, 1972), 95.

2. Bedini, *Life of Banneker*, 96; Needles, *An Historical Memoir*, 52.

3. John S. Tyson, *Life of Elisha Tyson, Philanthropist* (Baltimore: Benjamin Lundy, 1825), 19.

4. Monte A. Calvert, "The Abolition Society of Delaware, 1801-1807," *Delaware History* 10 (Oct. 1963): 300.

5. Mary Stoughton Locke, *Antislavery in America: From the Introduction to the Prohibition of the Slave Trade. 1619-1808* (1901; Gloucester, Mass.: Peter Smith, 1965), 99; Needles, *An Historical Memoir*, 52; Jesse Macy, *The Anti-Slavery Crusade: A Chronicle of the Gathering Storm* (New Haven: Yale University Press, 1919), 112.

6. Dwight L. Dumond, *Antislavery: The Crusade for Freedom in America* (Ann Arbor: Univ. of Michigan Press, 1961), 51-52.

7. Locke, *Antislavery in America*, 99.

8. H.M. Wagstaff, ed., *Minutes of the North Carolina Manumission Society, 1816-1834* (Chapel Hill: Univ. of North Carolina Press, 1934), 27.

9. Ibid., 100; Calvert, "Abolition Society of Delaware," 298.

10. Calvert, "Abolition Society of Delaware," p. 298.

11. Delaware Abolition Society (hereafter DAS), Minutes, 25 July 1817, HSP.

12. PAS, Minutes, 6 Jan. 1800, HSP.

13. Calvert, "Abolition Society of Delaware," 306.

14. American Convention of Abolition Societies, Minutes, 1817 Meeting (Philadelphia: Merritt, 1817), 13.

15. Locke, *Antislavery in America*, 100; Vincent P. Franklin, *The Education of Black Philadelphia: The Social and Educational History of a Minority Community, 1900-1950* (Philadelphia: Univ. of Pennsylvania Press, 1979), 5; Margaret Bacon, *History of the Pennsylvania Society for Promoting the Abolition of Slavery* (Philadelphia, Pennsylvania Abolition Society 1959), 2; Arthur Zilversmit, *The First Emancipation: The Abolition of Slavery in the North* (Chicago: Univ. of Chicago Press, 1967), 162.

16. W.E.B. Du Bois, *The Philadelphia Negro: A Social Study* (1899; New York: Benjamin Blom, 1967), 25.

17. Needles, *An Historical Memoir*, 13, 14.

18. James Brewer Stewart, *Holy Warriors: The Abolitionists and American Slavery* (New York: Hill and Wang, 1976), 14, 17, 18.

19. Ibid., 12-15; Jean R. Soderlund, *Quakers and Slavery: A Divided Spirit* (Princeton: Princeton Univ. Press, 1985), 3-4.

20. Zilversmit, *The First Emancipation*, 55; Jordan, *White Over Black*, 359; David Brion Davis, *The Problem of Slavery in the Age of the Revolution, 1770-1823* (Ithaca: Cornell Univ. Press, 1975), 216.

21. Edward Raymond Turner, *The Negro in Pennsylvania: Slavery, Servitude, Freedom, 1739-1861* (1911; New York: Negro Universities Press, 1969), 214.

22. Soderlund, *Quakers and Slavery*, 185.

23. Arna Bontemps, ed., *Great Slave Narratives* (Boston: Beacon Press, 1969), 89.

24. William P. Tilden, "Memorial Address Commemorating the 100th Anniversary of the Birth of Thomas Garrett," in James A. McGowen, *Station Master on the Underground Railroad: The Life and Letters of Thomas Garrett* (Moylan, Pa.: Whimsie Press, 1977), 25; Carol E. Hoffecker, *Delaware: A Bicentennial History* (New York: Norton, 1977), 99-100.

25. Levi Coffin, *Reminiscences of Levi Coffin* (1876 New York: Arno Press, 1968), 16-17.

26. Wiecek, *Sources of Antislavery*, 88; "Reports of the American Convention of Abolition Societies on Negroes and Slavery, Their

Appeals to Congress, and Their Addresses to the Citizens of the United States," *Journal of Negro History* 6 (July 1921): 321.

27. DAS Minutes, 18 July 1801, HSP; *Mirror of the Times and General Advertiser*, 8 Aug. 1801, 21 May 1806.

28. PAS Minutes, 26 Dec. 1822, HSP.

29. Jeffrey R. Brackett, *The Negro in Maryland: A Study of the Institution of Slavery* (Baltimore: Johns Hopkins Univ. Press, 1889), 184.

30. PAS Minutes, 7 Dec. 1811. HSP.

31. Ibid., 6 Jan. 1812.

32. Needles, *An Historical Memoir*, 67.

33. Hurd, *Laws of Freedom and Bondage* 2:70; Du Bois, *Philadelphia Negro*, 416.

34. Calvert, "Abolition Society of Delaware," 304.

35. Laws of the State of Delaware, 1797, vol. 2, 1093-95.

36. DAS Minutes, 2 May 1817, HSP.

37. Ibid., 4 July 1817.

38. Ibid.

39. Ibid., 21 Nov. 1817.

40. Petitions on Negroes and Slavery, 1817, in Delaware Legislative Papers, DHR.

41. James Bryan to Joseph Watson, JWP, HSP.

42. *Annals of Congress*, 14th Cong., 2d sess., 57-58; 15th Cong., 1st sess., 839.

43. American Convention of Abolition Societies, Minutes of the 1799 Meeting (Philadelphia: Poulson, 1800), 21-22.

44. American Convention Minutes, 1804 Meeting (Philadelphia: Solomon W. Conrad, 1804), 4-5.

45. "The Appeal of the American Convention of Abolition Societies to Anti-slavery groups," *Journal of Negro History* 6 (April 1921): 236; "Reports of the American Convention," 311, 361.

46. Memorial to Governor Mifflin, PAS Minutes, vol. 1 (1775-1800), 154-56, HSP.

47. Governor Mifflin's speech to the Pennsylvania legislature, 24 Aug. 1791, *Pennsylvania Archives*, series 4, vol. 4.

48. Ibid.; *United States Statutes*, vol. 1, 2d Congress, 2d sess., 302-5; Marion Gleason McDougall, *Fugitive Slaves, 1619-1865* (Boston: Ginn, 1891), 17; Campbell, *Slave-Catchers*, 7, 8, 10.

49. American Convention Minutes, 1797 Meeting (Philadelphia: Poulson, 1797), 38-39.

50. DAS Minutes, 21 Nov. 1803, HSD.
51. Ibid.
52. Ibid.
53. Ibid.
54. Child, *Isaac T. Hopper*, 83–84.
55. Ibid., 84–86.
56. Ibid., 86–87.
57. PAS, AC Minutes, 1 Jan. 1816, HSP.
58. Letter of John Kollock, 26 Aug. 1815, PAS, AC Minutes, HSP.
59. American Convention Minutes, 1798 Meeting (Philadelphia: Poulson, 1798), 12.
60. DAS Address to the American Convention, 25 July 1817 (copy), HSP.
61. PAS Minutes, 2 May 1794, 19 March 1821, HSP.
62. American Convention Minutes, 1799 Meeting (Philadelphia: Poulson, 1800), 9–10.
63. DAS Minutes, 21 Nov. 1817, 3 July 1818, HSP.
64. Locke, *Antislavery in America*, 94; American Convention Minutes, 1794 Meeting (Philadelphia: Poulson, 1794), 1.
65. Letter from (?) to Warner Mifflin, 16 Dec. 1810; from Mathew Neale to Warner Mifflin, 4 Jan. 1810; from Joseph Christy to Daniel Mifflin, 26 Oct. 1810; PAS Correspondence, Incoming, HSP.
66. PAS, AC Minutes, 24 Dec. 1788, HSP.
67. Ibid; letter of Governor Thomas Mifflin to Brigadier General Miro, 25 March 1789, *Pennsylvania Archives*, series 1, vol. 11, 567–68; PAS, AC Minutes, 2 Sept. 1789, HSP.
68. *Niles Register*, 25 Feb. 1826; *Signal of Liberty*, 16 March 1842.
69. *Signal of Liberty*, 16 March 1842; also Dumond, *Letters of James Gillespie Birney*, 651.
70. Winfield H. Collins, *The Domestic Slave-Trade of the Southern States* (Port Washington, N.Y.: Kennikat Press, 1904), 94–95.
71. PAS Minutes 1820-1847 and PAS AC Minutes, 1820-1842 HSP; Calvert, "Abolition Society of Delaware," 318.
72. Soderlund, *Quakers and Slavery*, 185.
73. American Convention Minutes, 1809 Meeting (Philadelphia: Bouvier, 1809), 7.
74. Stewart, *Holy Warriors*, 32–36; Lawrence J. Friedman, *Gregarious Saints: Self and Community in American Abolitionism, 1830-1870* (Cambridge: Cambridge Univ. Press, 1982). 1.

75. *Liberator*, 20 April 1833.

76. *Frederick Douglass' Paper*, 20 Aug. 1852, 2 June 1854.

77. For more on fugitive rescues, see Campbell, *Slave-Catchers*, 148-69.

78. Merton L. Dillon, *The Abolitionists: The Growth of A Dissenting Minority* (New York: Norton, 1974), 11; Jordan, *White Over Black*, 373.

79. Dillon, *The Abolitionists*, 18; Stewart, *Holy Warriors*, 29; Kenneth M. Stampp, *The Peculiar Institution: Slavery in the Antebellum South* (New York: Random House, 1956), 238-39; quote from Jordan, *White Over Black*, 348.

80. Dillon, *The Abolitionists*, 19, 20; Stewart, *Holy Warriors*, 29.

81. Edward Pessen, *Jacksonian America: Society, Personality and Politics* (Homewood, Ill.: Dorsey Press, 1969), 63, 157, 347-348, 350; Leon F. Litwack, *North of Slavery: The Negro in the Free States, 1790-1860* (Chicago: Univ. of Chicago Press, 1961), 75, 79, 82-83, 86, 91.

82. Dillon, *The Abolitionists*, 24. See also Leonard L. Richards, *"Gentlemen of Property and Standing": Anti-Abolition Mobs in Jacksonian America* (New York: Oxford Univ. Press, 1970).

83. Zilversmit, *First Emancipation*, 225; Dillon, *The Abolitionists*, 20; Jordan, *White Over Black*, 410; Nash, "Forging Freedom," 11; Philip S. Foner, "The Battle to End Discrimination Against Negroes on Philadelphia Streetcars," *Pennsylvania History* 40 (July 1973): 261.

84. Nash, "Forging Freedom," 3; Foner, "Battle to End Discrimination," 261.

85. Leonard P. Curry, *The Free Black in Urban America, 1800-1850: The Shadow of the Dream* (Chicago: Univ. of Chicago Press, 1981), 20.

86. Robert J. Cottrol, *The Afro-Yankees: Providence's Black Community in the Antebellum Era* (Westport, Conn.: Greenwood Press, 1982), 154-55.

87. Foner, "Battle to End Discrimination," 261.

88. Alexander Majoribanks, *Travels in South and North America* (London: Simpkin, Marshall, 1853), 435.

89. William Wells Brown, *The American Fugitive in Europe: Sketches of Places and People Abroad* (1855; New York: Negro Universities Press, 1969), 312.

90. Foner, "Battle to End Discrimination," 263; Theodore

Hershberg, "Free Blacks in Antebellum Philadelphia: A Study of Ex-slaves, Freeborn, and Socioeconomic Decline," *Journal of Social History* 5 (Winter 1971-72): 183.

91. Russell F. Weigley, *Philadelphia: A 300-Year History* (New York: W.W. Norton, 1982), 255; Bruce Laurie, *The Working People of Philadelphia, 1800-1850* (Philadelphia: Temple Univ. Press, 1980), 64-65; Davis, *Problem of Slavery*, 69.

92. Hershberg, "Free Blacks in Antebellum Philadelphia," 185, 187, 192.

93. Litwack, *North of Slavery*, 84-86.

94. Davis, *Problem of Slavery*, 69.

95. Turner, *Negro in Pennsylvania*, 247.

5. "An Almost Sleepless Vigilance": Black Resistance to Kidnapping

1. Gary B. Nash, *Forging Freedom: The Formation of Philadelphia's Black Community, 1720-1840* (Cambridge: Harvard Univ. Press, 1988). 5.

2. James Oliver Horton and Lois E. Horton, *Black Bostonians: Family Life and Community Struggle in the Antebellum North* (New York: Holmes and Meier, 1979), 100.

3. Curry, *The Free Black in Urban America*, 224-30.

4. Horton and Horton, *Black Bostonians*, 58, 97, 100.

5. "Queries Respecting the Slavery and Emancipation of Negroes in Massachusetts, Proposed by the Hon. Judge Tucker of Virginia, and Answered by the Rev. Dr. Belknap," *Massachusetts Historical Society Collections*, series 1, vol. 4 (1795), 204; "Protest Against Kidnapping and the Slave Trade, 1788," in Herbert Aptheker, ed. *A Documentary History of the Negro People of the United States*, vol. 1 (New York: Citadel Press, 1951), 20-21.

6. Horton and Horton, *Black Bostonians*, 29.

7. "Queries Respecting Slavery," 204-5; Aptheker, *Documentary History* 1:20-21.

8. Ibid.; Lorenzo J. Greene, "Prince Hall: Massachusetts Leader in Crisis." *Freedomways* 1 (Fall 1961): 253-54.

9. Aptheker, *Documentary History* 1:20-21. "Queries Respecting Slavery," 204-5, reports the blacks as being offered for sale and rescued by the governor on the Danish island of St. Bartholomew.

10. U.S. House of Representatives, *Reports*, no. 80, 1, 6-9. For more documents concerning the black sailors and the Negro sea-

men acts, see also Philip S. Foner and Ronald L. Lewis, eds., *The Black Worker to 1869* (Philadelphia: Temple Univ. Press, 1978), 1:196-236.

11. Nash, *Forging Freedom*, 2, 95-96, 98.

12. Herbert Aptheker, *"One Continual Cry": David Walker's Appeal to the Colored Citizens of the World, 1829-1830* (New York: Humanities Press, 1965), 29.

13. Albert J. Raboteau, "Richard Allen and the African Church Movement," in Leon Litwack and August Meier, eds., *Black Leaders of the Nineteenth Century* (Chicago: Univ. of Illinois Press, 1988), 2; Child, *Isaac T. Hopper*, 208-9; *National Anti-Slavery Standard*, 31 Dec. 1840.

14. Child, *Isaac Hopper*, 208-9; *National Anti-Slavery Standard*, 31 December 1840.

15. Carol V. George, *Segregated Sabbaths: Richard Allen and the Emergence of the Independent Black Churches, 1760-1840* (New York: Oxford Univ. Press, 1978), 4.

16. Petition of Absalom Jones and others to Congress, 2 Jan. 1800, NA. The petition is also reprinted in Parrish, *Remarks on the Slavery of Black People*, 49-51, although Parrish dates the document 30 Dec. 1799.

17. *Annals of Congress*, 6th Cong., 1st sess., 229-33.

18. Ibid., 233-45.

19. Report of the committee referred the petition of Jones and others, NA.

20. *Annals of Congress*, 6th Cong., 2d sess., 1034, 1045; 7th Cong., 1st sess., 336, 423, 425.

21. W.O. Blake, *The History of Slavery and the Slave Trade, Ancient and Modern* (Columbus, Ohio: H. Miller, 1860), 424, *Annals of Congress*, 4th Cong., 2d sess., 2015-23; Aptheker, *A Documentary History*, 1:39. The petition is also reprinted in Aptheker, *A Documentary History* 1:39-44, and in Parrish, *Remarks on the Slavery of Black People*, appendix.

22. *Annals of Congress*, 4th Cong. 2d sess., 2015-23.

23. *Annals of Congress*, 5th Cong. 1st sess., 656-70, 945, 1021-33; Blake, *History of Slavery*, p. 445; Hurd, *The Laws of Freedom and Bondage*, 2, p. 85. Both petitions are reprinted in Parrish, *Remarks on the Slavery of Black People*, 54-56, which also contains court records from the case.

24. Foner and Lewis, *The Black Worker* 1:296-314.

25. Foner, *History of Black Americans* 3:25-26.

26. Benjamin Quarles, *Black Abolitionists* (New York: Oxford Univ. Press, 1969), 150.

27. Ibid., 154; *First Annual Report of the New York Committee of Vigilance* (New York: Percy and Reed, 1837), 13-14.

28. *Report of the Vigilance Committee*, 3.

29. Ibid, pp. 13-14; Quarles, *Black Abolitionists*, 154; Jane Pease and William Pease, *They Who Would Be Free: Blacks' Search for Freedom, 1830-1861* (New York: Atheneum, 1974), 212.

30. Dorothy B. Porter, "David M. Ruggles, an Apostle of Human Rights," *Journal of Negro History* 27 (Jan. 1943): 25, 27, 30, 33.

31. *Report of the Vigilance Committee*, 73-77.

32. *Liberator*, 5 Oct. 1838.

33. *Report of the Vigilance Committee*, 7.

34. Pease and Pease, *They Who Would Be Free*, 212.

35. Foner, *History of Black Americans* 3:20.

36. William Still, *The Underground Railroad* (Philadelphia: People's Publishing, 1872), 348.

37. Frederick Douglass, *Narrative of the Life of Frederick Douglass, An American Slave* (1845; New York: Signet, 1968), 117.

38. *Frederick Douglass' Paper*, 2 June 1854.

39. Roi Ottley and William Weatherby, eds., *The Negro in New York: An Informal Social History* (New York: New York Public Library, 1967), 80, 87.

40. For more on the Christiana Riot, see Jonathan Katz, *Resistance at Christiana: The Fugitive Slave Rebellion, Christiana, Pennsylvania, September 11, 1851: A Documentary Account* (New York: Thomas Y. Crowell, 1974), and Thomas P. Slaughter, *Bloody Dawn: The Christiana Riot and Racial Violence in the Antebellum North* (New York: Oxford Univ. Press, 1991).

41. William Parker, "The Freedman's Story," *Atlantic Monthly* 17 (Feb. 1866): 162.

42. Ibid., 160-61.

43. Slaughter, *Bloody Dawn*, 44. The gang's name comes from Gap Hills, where members lived, as well as the Gap Tavern, which they frequented.

44. W.U. Hensel, *The Christiana Riot and the Treason Trials of 1851* (Lancaster, Pa.: New Era Printing, 1911), 15; Franklin Ellis and Samuel Evans, *History of Lancaster County, Pennsylvania* (Philadelphia: Everts and Peck, 1883), 1:71.

45. Parker, "The Freedman's Story," 161-66.

46. Ibid.

47. Foner, *History of Black Americans*, vol. 3, 30.

48. *Anglo-African Magazine*, June 1859; Philip S. Foner, ed., *The Voice of Black America: Major Speeches By Negroes in the United States, 1797-1971* (New York: Simon and Schuster, 1972), 208-15.

Conclusion

1. *Northern Star and Freedman's Advocate* (Albany), 17 March 1842.

2. Winfield Collins, *The Domestic Slave-Trade of the Southern States* (Port Washington, N.Y.: Kennikat Press, 1904), 94-95.

3. Report of the Vigilance Committee, 7.

4. Berlin, *Slaves Without Masters*.

5. Julie Winch, "Philadelphia and the Other Underground Railroad." *Pennsylvania Magazine of History and Biography* 111 (Jan. 1987): 3.

6. Billy G. Smith and Richard Wojtowicz, "The Precarious Freedom of Blacks in the Mid-Atlantic Region: Excerpts from the Pennsylvania Gazette, 1728-1776," *Pennsylvania Magazine of History and Biography* 113 (April 1989): 237.

7. *African Observer*, July 1827.

8. Edmund S. Morgan, *American Slavery, American Freedom: The Ordeal of Colonial Virginia* (New York: W.W. Norton, 1975); William W. Freehling, "The Founding Fathers and Slavery," *American Historical Review* 77 (Feb. 1972): 380-85.

9. Robert L. Zangrando, *The NAACP Crusade Against Lynching, 1909-1950* (Philadelphia: Temple Univ. Press, 1980), 210.

Bibliography

Primary Sources, Unpublished

Brooke County Court Records, West Virginia Collection, West Virginia University, Morgantown

Salmon P. Chase Papers, Ohio Historical Society, Columbus

Committee on the District of Columbia Folder, 6 February 1844, to 10 December 1844, Senate 28A-G3, National Archives, Washington, D.C.

Committee on the Judiciary Petitions—Protection of Free Colored Citizens within the Jurisdiction of the several slave states, 3 March-18 March 1854, HR33A-G10.8, National Archives, Washington, D.C.

Delaware Abolition Society, Minutes, Delaware Historical Society, Wilmington

Delaware Abolition Society, Minutes, Historical Society of Pennsylvania, Philadelphia

Delaware Legislative Papers, Delaware Hall of Records, Dover

Helen S. Garrett Papers, Delaware Historical Society, Wilmington

Ralph Leete Papers, Western Reserve Historical Society, Cleveland

Louisville Chancery Court Records (copies), Kentucky Department for Libraries and Archives, Frankfort

Miscellaneous Papers, 1655-1805, 3 Lower Counties Delaware, Historical Society of Pennsylvania, Philadelphia

Monongalia County Court Records, West Virginia Collection, West Virginia University, Morgantown

"Negroes Kidnapped" in General Reference no. 706, Delaware Hall of Records, Dover

Pennsylvania Abolition Society, Acting Committee Minutes, Historical Society of Pennsylvania, Philadelphia.

Pennsylvania Abolition Society, Incoming Correspondence, Historical Society of Pennsylvania, Philadelphia.

Petition of Absalom Jones and others, 2 January 1800, HR6A-F4.2, National Archives, Washington, D.C.

Philadelphia County Court Records (copies), City Hall, Philadelphia

Peyton Polly Papers, Ohio Historical Society, Columbus

Select Committee on the African Slave Trade, Papers, HR14A-C17.4, National Archives, Washington, D.C.

Select Committee to Inquire into the Existence of an Inhuman and Illegal Traffic in Slaves . . . in the District of Columbia, Papers, HR14A-C17.4, National Archives, Washington, D.C.

William Seward Papers (copies), University of Rochester Library, Rochester, N.Y.

Slaves and Slavery, Papers 1797–1826, 1860, West Virginia Collection, West Virginia University, Morgantown

Sussex County Court Records, Delaware Hall of Records, Dover

Vigilant Committee of Philadelphia, Minutes, Historical Society of Pennsylvania, Philadelphia

Joseph Watson Papers, Historical Society of Pennsylvania, Philadelphia

Reuben Wood Papers, Ohio Historical Society, Columbus

Primary Sources, Published

NEWSPAPERS

African Observer (Philadelphia)

The African Repository (Washington, D.C.)

Albany (New York) *Evening Journal*

American Anti-Slavery Reporter (New York)

The Anglo-African Magazine (New York)

Ann Arbor (Michigan) *Local News*

Anti-Slavery Advocate (London)

Anti-Slavery Bugle (Salem, Ohio)

Anti-Slavery Record (New York)

Baltimore Sun

Cairo (Illinois) *Weekly Times and Delta*

Centinel of Freedom (Newark, N.J.)

Chester County (Pennsylvania) *Times*

Chicago Tribune

Cincinnati Gazette

Cincinnati Herald

Cleveland Leader

The Colombian Mirror and Alexandria Gazette (Virginia)

The Colored American

Cortland Republican (New York)
Courier and Enquirer (Concord, N.H.)
Daily Delta (New Orleans)
Daily Sun (Columbus, Georgia)
Delaware Gazette and American Watchman
Delaware State Journal
Delaware State News
Democratic Press (Philadelphia)
Detroit Advertiser
Edwardsville Journal (Illinois)
Emancipator (New York)
Federal Gazette and Philadelphia Evening Post
Floridian and Journal (Tallahassee)
Frankfort Yeoman (Kentucky)
Frederick Douglass' Paper (Rochester, N.Y.)
Genius of Universal Emancipation (Washington, D.C.)
Grand Gulf Advertiser (Mississippi)
Greensburg Gazette (Pennsylvania)
Hazard's Register of Pennsylvania
Indiana Free Democrat
Lawrence Republican (Kansas)
Leeds Mercury (England)
Liberator (Boston)
The Liberty Bell (Boston)
Memphis Enquirer
Milford News (Delaware)
Mirror of the Times and General Advertiser (Wilmington)
Missouri Democrat
Mobile Register
Montreal Gazette
Natchez Weekly Chronicle
National Anti-Slavery Standard (New York)
National Intelligencer (Washington, D.C.)
New Albany Tribune
New York Evening Post
New York Times
New York Transcript
New York Tribune
New York Weekly Mercury
New Bern Spectator (North Carolina)

Niles' National Register (Baltimore)
The Non-Slaveholder (Philadelphia)
North American and United States Gazette (Philadelphia)
The North Star (Rochester, N.Y.)
Northern Star and Freedman's Advocate (Albany)
Opelousas Patriot (Louisiana)
Ottawa Free Trader (Illinois)
Pennsylvania Freeman
Pennsylvania Gazette
Philadelphia Gazette
Philadelphia Sunday Dispatch
The Philanthropist (Cincinnati)
Poulson's Daily Advertiser (Philadelphia)
Richmond Daily Dispatch
St. Louis Daily Missouri Democrat
Shawneetown Illinoian
Signal of Liberty (Ann Arbor)
Southern Argus and Lowndes County (Columbia, Mississippi)
Spectator (Edwardsville, Illinois)
Vicksburg Register
Village Record (West Chester, Pennsylvania)
Voice of the Fugitive (Sandwich, Canada West)
Western Citizen (Chicago)
Western Spy (Cincinnati)
Wilmington Journal Every Evening
Woodville Republican (Mississippi)

SLAVE NARRATIVES

Allen, Richard. *The Life, Experience and Gospel Labors of the Rt. Rev. Richard Allen.* Philadelphia: Lee and Yeocum, 1887.
Andrews, William L., ed. *Sisters of the Spirit: Three Black Women's Autobiographies of the Nineteenth Century.* Bloomington, Ind.: Indiana Univ. Press, 1986.
———. *To Tell a Free Story: The First Century of Afro-American Autobiography, 1760-1865.* Urbana: Univ. of Illinois Press, 1986.
Bayliss, John F., ed. *Black Slave Narratives.* New York: MacMillan, 1970.
Bibb, Henry. *Narrative of the Life and Adventures of Henry Bibb, an American Slave.* New York: Privately published, 1849.
Blassingame, John W., ed. *Slave Testimony: Two Centuries of Letters,*

Speeches, Interviews, and Autobiographies. Baton Rouge: Louisiana State Univ. Press, 1977.

Bontemps, Arna, ed. *Five Black Lives*. Middleton, Conn.: Wesleyan University Press, 1971.

————. *Great Slave Narratives*. Boston: Beacon Press, 1969.

Botkin, B.A., ed. *Lay My Burden Down: A Folk History of Slavery*. Chicago: Univ. of Chicago Press, 1945.

Brown, John. *Slave Life in Georgia: A Narrative of the Life, Suffering, and Escape of John Brown, a Fugitive Slave*. London: W.M. Watts, 1855.

Clarke, Lewis. *Narrative of the Sufferings of Lewis Clarke during a Captivity of More Than Twenty-Five Years among the Algerines of Kentucky*. Boston: David H. Ela, 1845.

Davis, Noah. *A Narrative of the Life of Rev. Noah Davis. A Colored Man*. Baltimore: John F. Weishampel, 1859.

Douglass, Frederick. *Narrative of the Life of Frederick Douglass: An American Slave*. 1845. Reprint. New York: Signet, 1968.

Drew, Benjamin, ed. *The Refugee: Narratives of Fugitive Slaves in Canada*. Boston: John Jewett, 1856.

Green, William. *Narrative of Events in the Life of William Green*. Springfield, Mass.: L.M. Guernsey, 1853.

Griffiths, Mattie. *Autobiography of a Female Slave*. 1858. Reprint. New York: Negro Universities Press, 1969.

Hawkins, William G. *Lunsford Lane; or, Another Helper from North Carolina*. 1863. Reprint. New York: Negro Universities Press, 1969.

Henson, Josiah. *Father Henson's Story of His Own Life*. Boston: John P. Jewett, 1858.

Hughes, Louis. *Thirty Years a Slave*. 1867. Reprint. New York: Negro Universities Press, 1969.

Jefferson, Isaac. *Memoirs of a Monticello Slave*. Charlottesville: Univ. of Virginia Press, 1951.

Jones, Thomas H. *The Experience of Thomas Jones, Who Was a Slave for Forty-Three Years*. Worcester, Mass.: Henry J. Howland, 1857.

Katz, William L., ed. *Five Slave Narratives*. New York: Arno Press, 1968.

Keckley, Elizabeth. *Behind the Scenes: Thirty Years a Slave and Four Years in the White House*. 1868. Reprint. New York: Arno Press, 1968.

Lane, Lunsford. *The Narrative of Lunsford Lane*. Boston: Privately published, 1842.

Loguen, J. W. *The Reverend J. W. Loguen as a Slave and as a Free Man.* 1859. Reprint. New York: Negro Universities Press, 1968.

Nichols, Charles H., ed. *Black Men in Chains: Narratives by Escaped Slaves.* New York: L. Hill, 1972.

————. *Many Thousand Gone: The Ex-slaves' Accounts of Their Bondage and Freedom.* Leiden: E.J. Brill, 1963.

Northup, Solomon. *Twelve Years a Slave.* London: Miller, Orton, and Mulligan, 1854.

Osofsky, Gilbert. *Puttin' on Ole Massa: The Slave Narratives of Henry Bibb, William Wells Brown, and Solomon Northup.* New York: Harper and Row, 1969.

Pickard, Kate E. R. *The Kidnapped and Ransomed.* 1856. Reprint. New York: Negro Universities Press, 1968.

Randolph, Peter. *Sketches of Slave Life.* Boston: Privately printed, 1855.

Rawick, George W., ed. *The American Slave: A Composite Autobiography.* Westport, Conn.: Greenwood Press, 1972.

Roper, Moses. *A Narrative of the Adventures and Escape of Moses Roper from American Slavery.* 1838. Reprint. New York: Negro Universities Press, 1970.

Steward, Austin. *Twenty-Two Years a Slave and Forty Years a Freeman.* Rochester, N.Y.: William Alling, 1857.

Williams, James. *Narrative of James Williams, an American Slave.* New York: American Anti-Slavery Society, 1838.

Yetman, Norman, ed. *Life Under the "Peculiar Institution": Selections from the Slave Narrative Collection.* Huntington, N.Y.: Robert Krieger, 1976.

————. *Voices From Slavery.* New York: Holt and Rinehart, 1970.

PUBLISHED PRIMARY SOURCES, MISCELLANEOUS

"Advice Given Negroes a Century Ago." *Journal of Negro History* 6 (Jan. 1921): 103-12.

Alexander, James Edward. *Transatlantic Sketches, Comprising Visits to the Most Interesting Scenes in North America and West Indies.* 2 vols. London: R. Bently, 1833.

American Anti-Slavery Society. Annual Reports 1-6, 1834-39.

American Convention of Abolition Societies. Minutes of Proceedings, 1794-1839.

American Society of Free Persons of Colour: Constitution and Address by Richard Allen. 1831. Reprint. Philadelphia: Rhistoric Publications, 1969.

American State Papers, Class X, Misc. vol 1. Washington, D.C., 1834.

Annals: The Debates and Proceedings in the Congress of the United States. Washington, D.C., 1789–1824.

"The Appeal of the American Convention of Abolition Societies to Anti-slavery Groups." *Journal of Negro History* 6 (April 1921): 200–40.

Aptheker, Herbert, ed. *A Documentary History of the Negro People of the United States.* 4 vols. New York: Citadel Press, 1951.

Blaustein, Albert P., and Zangrando, Robert L., eds. *Civil Rights and the Black American: A Documentary History.* 2d ed. Chicago: Northwestern Univ. Press, 1991.

Brissot de Warville, J. P. *New Travels in the United States of America, 1788.* Translated by Mara Soceanu Vamos and Durand Echeverria; edited by Durand Echeverria. 1791. Reprint. Cambridge: Harvard University Press, 1964.

Brown, William Wells. *The American Fugitive in Europe: Sketches of People and Places Abroad.* 1855. Reprint. New York, Negro Universities Press, 1969.

Browne, Peter A. *A Review of the Trial, Conviction, and Sentence of George F. Alberti, for Kidnapping.* Philadelphia, 1851; Historical Society of Pennsylvania.

Buckingham, James S. *The Eastern and Western States of America.* 2 vols. London: Fisher and Son, 1842.

Child, Lydia Maria. *An Appeal in Favor of that Class of Americans Called Africans.* Boston: Ticknor and Son, 1833.

———. *The Duty of Disobedience to the Fugitive Slave Law: An Appeal to the Legislators of Massachusetts.* Boston: American Anti-Slavery Society, 1860.

Coffin, Levi. *Reminiscences of Levi Coffin.* 1876. Reprint. New York: Arno Press, 1968.

Congressional Debates. Washington, D.C. 1825–37.

Congressional Globe. Washington, D.C., 1833–60.

Delaware, State of. Laws. Vol. 2. 1797.

Donnan, Elizabeth, ed. *Documents Illustrative of the History of the Slave Trade in America.* 3 vols. Washington, D.C.: Carnegie Institute, 1930–35.

Dumond, Dwight L., ed. *Letters of James Gillespie Birney. 1831–1857.* 2 vols. 1938. Reprint. Gloucester, Mass.: Peter Smith, 1966.

Farrand, Max, ed. *The Records of the Federal Convention of 1787.* 3 vols. New Haven: Yale Univ. Press. 1911.

The First Annual Report of the New York Committee of Vigilance. New York: Percy and Reed, 1837.

Foner, Philip S., ed. *The Voice of Black America: Major Speeches by Negroes in the United States, 1797-1971.* New York: Simon and Schuster, 1972.

Foner, Philip S., and Walker, George E., eds. *Proceedings of the Black State Conventions, 1840-1865.* 2 vols. Philadelphia: Temple Univ. Press, 1979–80.

Foner, Philip S., and Lewis, Ronald L., eds. *The Black Worker to 1869.* Vol 1. Philadelphia: Temple University Press, 1978.

Harrison, Eliza Cope, ed. *Philadelphia Merchant: The Diary of Thomas P. Cope, 1800-1851.* South Bend, Ind.: Gateway Editions, 1978.

Haviland, Laura. *A Woman's Life Work in the Underground Railroad and the Civil War.* Chicago: C.V. Waite, 1881.

House Reports. Nos. 27, 119 (1842), no. 80 (1843). Washington, D.C.

Hurd, John C. *The Laws of Freedom and Bondage in the United States.* 2 vols. Boston: Little, Brown, 1858-59.

Journal of the House of Representatives. Washington, D.C., 1791, 1843.

Journal of the Senate. Washington, D.C., 1792, 1843.

Majoribanks, Alexander. *Travels in South and North America.* London: Simpkin, Marshall, 1853.

May, Samuel. *The Fugitive Slave Law and Its Victims.* Revised and enlarged ed. New York: American Anti-Slavery Society, 1861.

McConnel, George Murray. "Illinois and Its People." *Transactions of the Illinois Historical Society,* no. 7. Springfield, Ill., 1902.

Narrative and Confessions of Lucretia P. Cannon. New York, 1841; Historical Society of Delaware.

Palfrey, John G. "Letter to a Whig Neighbor, on the Approaching State Election, by an Old Conservative," Boston: Crosby, Nichols, 1855.

Parker, William. "The Freedman's Story." *Atlantic Monthly* 17 (Feb. 1866): 152-66; (March 1866): 276-95.

Parrish, John. *Remarks on the Slavery of Black People.* Philadelphia: Kimber, Conrad, 1806.

Pennsylvania Archives: Governor's Papers, series 4. 12 vols. Harrisburg, Pa.: William Stanley Ray, 1900-1902.

Phillips, Wendell. "Argument of Wendell Phillips, Esq. against the Repeal of the Personal Liberty Law, before the Committee of the Legislature, Tuesday, January 19, 1861." Boston: R.F. Wallcutt,

1861, in *Anti-Slavery Tracts*, series 2 (nos. 15–25), 1861 Westport, Conn.: Negro Universities Press, 1970.

"Queries Respecting the Slavery and Emancipation of Negroes in Massachusetts, Proposed by the Hon. Judge Tucker of Virginia, and Answered By the Rev. Dr. Belknap (1795)." *Massachusetts Historical Society Collections*. Series 1, vol 4.

"Reports of the American Convention of Abolition Societies on Negroes and Slavery, Their Appeals to Congress, and Their Addresses to the Citizens of the United States." *Journal of Negro History* 6 (July 1921): 310–74.

Ripley, C. Peter, and Finkenbine, Roy E., eds. *The Black Abolitionist Papers*. Vol. 2, *Canada, 1830-1865*. Chapel Hill: Univ. of North Carolina Press, 1986.

Ripley, C. Peter, and Rossbach, Jeffrey S., eds. *The Black Abolitionist Papers*. Vol. 1, *British Isles, 1830-1865*. Chapel Hill: Univ. of North Carolina Press, 1985.

"Samuel Hoar's Expulsion from Charleston." *Old South Leaflets*, no. 140. Boston: Directors of the Old South Work, n.d.

Smith, Billy G., and Wojtowicz, Richard. *Blacks Who Stole Themselves: Advertisements for Runaways in the Pennsylvania Gazette, 1728-1790*. Philadelphia: Univ. of Pennsylvania Press, 1989.

————. "The Precarious Freedom of Blacks in the Mid–Atlantic Region: Excerpts from the *Pennsylvania Gazette*, 1728–1776." *Pennsylvania Magazine of History and Biography* 113 (April 1989): 237–64.

Still, William. *The Underground Railroad*. Philadelphia: People's Publishing, 1872.

Torrey, Jesse. *American Slave-Trade*. 1822. Reprint. New York: Negro Universities Press, 1970.

————. *A Portraiture of Domestic Slavery in the United States*. 2d ed. Ballston Spa, N.Y.: Privately printed, 1818.

U.S. Bureau of the Census. *Negro Population in the United States. 1790-1915*. Washington, D.C.: G.P.O., 1918.

United States Statutes at Large. Boston: Little Brown, 1789-1851.

Wagstaff, H.M., ed. *Minutes of the North Carolina Manumission Society, 1816-1834*. Chapel Hill: Univ. of North Carolina Press, 1934.

Secondary Sources

BOOKS

Angle, Paul M., and Miers, Earl Schenk, *Tragic Years, 1860-1865*. Vol. 2. New York: Simon and Schuster, 1960.

Aptheker, Herbert. *"One Continual Cry": David Walker's Appeal to the Colored Citizens of the World. 1829-1830.* New York: Humanities Press, 1965.

Bacon, Margaret. *History of the Pennsylvania Society for Promoting the Abolition of Slavery.* Philadelphia, Pennsylvania Abolition Society 1959.

Bedini, Silvio A. *The Life of Benjamin Banneker.* New York: Charles Scribner's Sons, 1972.

Berlin, Ira. *Slaves Without Masters: The Free Negro in the Antebellum South.* New York: Pantheon Books, 1974.

Berry, Mary Frances, and John W. Blassingame. *Long Memory: The Black Experience in America.* New York: Oxford Univ. Press, 1982.

Blake, W.O. *The History of Slavery and the Slave Trade, Ancient and Modern.* Columbus, Ohio: H. Miller, 1860.

Blassingame, John W. *The Slave Community: Plantation Life in the Antebellum South.* New York: Oxford Univ. Press, 1979.

Blockson, Charles L. *The Underground Railroad in Pennsylvania.* Jacksonville, N.C.: Flame International, 1981.

Blue, Frederick J. *Salmon P. Chase: A Life in Politics.* Kent, Ohio: Kent State Univ. Press, 1987.

Brackett, Jeffrey R. *The Negro in Maryland: A Study of the Institution of Slavery.* Baltimore: Johns Hopkins Univ. Press, 1889.

Breen, T.H. and Stephen Innes, *Myne Own Ground: Race Freedom on Virginia's Eastern Shore, 1640-1676.* New York: Oxford Univ. Press, 1980.

Brown, Letitia Woods. *Free Negroes in the District of Columbia, 1790-1846.* New York: Oxford Univ. Press, 1972.

Campbell, Stanley W. *The Slave-Catchers: Enforcement of the Fugitive Slave Law, 1850-1860.* Chapel Hill: Univ. of North Carolina Press, 1970.

Cheek, William, and Cheek, Aimee Lee. *John Mercer Langston and the Fight for Black Freedom, 1829-1865.* Champaign: University of Illinois Press, 1989.

Child, Lydia Maria. *Isaac T. Hopper: A True Life.* Boston, John P. Jewett, 1853.

Cobb, Thomas R. R. *An Inquiry into the Law of Slavery in the United States.* Philadelphia: Johnson, 1858.

Coddington, Edwin B. *The Gettysburg Campaign: A Study in Command.* N.Y.: Charles Scribner's Sons, 1968.

Coleman, J. Winston. *Slavery Times in Kentucky.* Chapel Hill: Univ. of North Carolina Press, 1940.

Collins, Winfield H. *The Domestic Slave-Trade of the Southern States.* Port Washington, N.Y.: Kennikat Press, 1904.

Cottrol, Robert J. *Afro-Yankees: Providence's Free Black Community in the Antebellum Era.* Westport, Conn.: Greenwood, 1982.

Crete, Liliane. *Daily Life in Louisiana, 1815-1830.* Baton Rouge, 1978.

Curry, Leonard. *The Free Black in Urban America, 1800-1850.* Chicago: Univ. of Chicago Press, 1981.

Curtin, Philip D. *The Atlantic Slave Trade: A Census.* Madison: Univ. of Wisconsin Press, 1969.

Davis, David Brion. *The Problem of Slavery in the Age of the Revolution, 1770-1823.* Ithaca: Cornell Univ. Press, 1975.

Degler, Carl N. *Neither Black Nor White: Slavery and Race Relations in Brazil and the United States.* New York: Macmillan, 1971.

Dillon, Merton L. *The Abolitionists: The Growth of a Dissenting Minority.* New York: W.W. Norton, 1974.

Du Bois, W.E.B. *The Philadelphia Negro: A Social Study.* 1899. Reprint. New York: Benjamin Blom, 1967.

Dumond, Dwight L. *Antislavery: The Crusade for Freedom in America.* Ann Arbor: Univ. of Michigan Press, 1961.

Ellis, Franklin, and Evans, Samuel. *History of Lancaster County, Pennsylvania.* Philadelphia: Everts and Peck, 1883.

Fehrenbacher, Don E. *The Dred Scott Case: Its Significance in American Law and Politics.* New York: Oxford Univ. Press, 1978.

Fields, Barbara Jeanne. *Slavery and Freedom on the Middle Ground: Maryland During the Nineteenth Century.* New Haven: Yale University Press, 1985.

Finkelman, Paul. *An Imperfect Union: Slavery, Federalism, and Comity.* Chapel Hill: Univ. of North Carolina Press, 1980.

————. *The Law of Freedom and Bondage: A Casebook.* New York: Oceana Publications, 1986.

————. "Slavery and the Constitutional Convention: Making a Covenant with Death." In *Beyond Confederation: Origins of the Constitution and American National Identity*, pp. 188-225. Edited by Richard Beeman, Stephen Botein, and Edward C. Carter, III. Chapel Hill: Univ. of North Carolina Press, 1987.

————. *Slavery in the Courtroom: An Annotated Bibliography of American Cases.* Washington, D.C.: Library of Congress, 1985.

Foner, Eric. *Free Soil, Free Labor, Free Men: The Ideology of the Republican Party before the Civil War.* New York: Oxford Univ. Press, 1970.

Foner, Philip S. *History of Black Americans*. 3 vols. Westport, Conn.: Greenwood Press, 1983.

Franklin, John Hope. *The Free Negro in North Carolina*. Chapel Hill: Univ. of North Carolina, 1943.

————. *A Southern Odyssey: Travelers in the Antebellum North*. Baton Rouge: Louisiana State Univ. Press, 1976.

Franklin, Vincent P. *The Education of Black Philadelphia: The Social and Educational History of a Minority Community, 1900-1950*. Philadelphia: Univ. of Pennsylvania Press, 1979.

Friedman, Lawrence J. *Gregarious Saints: Self and Community in American Abolitionism, 1830-1870*. Cambridge: Cambridge Univ. Press, 1982.

Gara, Larry. *The Liberty Line: The Legend of the Underground Railroad*. Lexington: Univ. of Kentucky Press, 1966.

George, Carol V. *Segregated Sabbaths: Richard Allen and the Emergence of the Independent Black Churches, 1760-1840*. New York: Oxford Univ. Press, 1978.

Giles, Ted. *Patty Cannon: Woman of Mystery*. Easton, Md.: Easton Publishing, 1965.

The Governors of Ohio. 2d ed. Columbus: Ohio Historical Society, 1969.

Greene, Lorenzo J. *The Negro in Colonial New England, 1620-1776*. Port Washington, N.Y.: Kennikat Press, 1966.

Harris, N. Dwight. *The History of Negro Servitude in Illinois, 1719-1864*. 1904. Reprint. New York: Negro Universities Press, 1969.

Hazzard, Robert. *The History of Seaford*. Seaford, Delaware: Privately printed, 1899.

Hensel, W.U. *The Christiana Riot and the Treason Trials of 1851*. Lancaster, Pa.: New Era Printing, 1911.

Hoffecker, Carol E. *Delaware: A Bicentennial History*. New York: W.W. Norton, 1977.

————. *Wilmington, Delaware: Portrait of an Industrial City, 1830-1910*. Charlottesville: Univ. of Virginia Press, 1974.

Horton, James O., and Horton, Lois E. *Black Bostonians: Family Life and Community Struggle in the Antebellum North*. New York: Holmes and Meier, 1979.

Horton, James O. *Free People of Color: Inside the African American Community*. Washington, D.C.: Smithsonian Institution Press, 1993.

Hyman, Harold M., and Wiecek, William M. *Equal Justice under the*

Law: Constitutional Development, 1835-1875. New York: Harper and Row, 1982.

Ireland, Robert M. *The County Courts in Antebellum Kentucky.* Lexington: Univ. of Kentucky Press, 1972.

Jackson, W. A. *History of the Trial of Castner Hanaway and Others for Treason.* Philadelphia, U. Hunt and Sons, 1852.

Johnson, Guion. *Ante-bellum North Carolina: A Social History.* Chapel Hill: Univ. of North Carolina Press, 1937.

Johnson, Robert C. "The Transportation of Vagrant Children from London to Virginia, 1618-1622," pp. 137-156 *Early Stuart Studies,* ed. H.S. Reinmuth, Jr. Minneapolis: Univ. of Minnesota Press, 1970.

Jordan, Winthrop. *White Over Black: American Attitudes toward the Negro, 1550-1812.* Chapel Hill: Univ. of North Carolina Press, 1968.

Katz, Jonathan. *Resistance at Christiana: The Fugitive Slave Rebellion, Christiana, Pennsylvania, September 11, 1851: A Documentary Account.* New York: Thomas Y. Crowell, 1974.

Laurie, Bruce. *The Working People of Philadelphia, 1800-1850.* Philadelphia: Temple Univ. Press, 1980.

Levy, Leonard W. *Original Intent and the Framers' Constitution.* New York: Macmillan, 1988.

Litwack, Leon F. *North of Slavery: The Negro in the Free States.* Chicago: Univ. of Chicago Press, 1961.

Locke, Mary Stoughton. *Anti-Slavery in America: From the Introduction to the Prohibition of the Slave Trade, 1619-1808.* 1901. Reprint. Gloucester, Mass.: Peter Smith, 1965.

Lynd, Staughton. *Class Conflict, Slavery and the United States Constitution.* New York: Bobbs–Merrill, 1967.

Macy, Jesse. *The Anti-Slavery Crusade: A Chronicle of the Gathering Storm.* New Haven: Yale Univ. Press, 1919.

McDougall, Marion Gleason. *Fugitive Slaves, 1619-1865.* Boston: Ginn and Company, 1891.

McGowan, James A. *The Station Master on the Underground Railroad: The Life and Letters of Thomas Garrett.* Moylan, Pa.: Whimsie Press, 1977.

McKivigan, John R. *The War against Proslavery Religion: Abolitionism and the Northern Churches, 1830-1865.* Ithaca: Cornell Univ. Press, 1984.

McManus, Edgar J. *Black Bondage in the North.* Syracuse: Syracuse Univ. Press, 1973.

————. *A History of Negro Slavery in New York*. Syracuse: Syracuse Univ. Press, 1966.

McPherson, James M. *The Negro's Civil War*. 1965.

Merrill, Walter M. *Against Wind and Tide: A Biography of William Lloyd Garrison*. Cambridge: Harvard Univ. Press, 1963.

Messenger, R.W. *Patty Cannon Administers Justice, or Joe Johnson's Last Kidnapping Exploit*. 1926. Reprint. Cambridge, Md.: Tidewater Publishing, 1960.

Middleton, Stephen. *Ohio and the Antislavery Activities of Salmon Portland Chase, 1830-49*. New York: Garland, 1990.

Mitchell, Reid. *Civil War Soldiers*. New York: Viking, 1988.

Morgan, Edmund S. *American Slavery, American Freedom: The Ordeal of Colonial Virginia*. New York: W.W. Norton, 1975.

Morris, Thomas D. *Free Men All: The Personal Liberty Laws of the North, 1780-1861*. Baltimore: Johns Hopkins Univ. Press, 1974.

Mullin, Gerald W. *Flight and Rebellion: Slave Resistance in Eighteenth Century Virginia*. New York: Oxford Univ. Press, 1972.

Nash, Gary B. *Forging Freedom: The Formation of Philadelphia's Black Community, 1720-1840*. Cambridge: Harvard Univ. Press, 1988.

————. "Forging Freedom: The Emancipation Experience in the Northern Seaport Cities, 1775-1820." In *Slavery and Freedom in the Age of the American Revolution*, pp. 3–48. Edited by Ira Berlin and Ronald Hoffman. Charlottesville: Univ. of Virginia Press, 1983.

Needles, Edward. *An Historical Memoir of the Pennsylvania Society for Promoting the Abolition of Slavery*. 1848. Reprint. New York: Arno Press and New York Times, 1969.

Nye, Russel B. *Unfettered Freedom: Civil Liberties and the Slavery Controversy, 1830-1860*. East Lansing: Michigan State College Press, 1949.

Ottley, Roi, and William Weatherby, eds. *The Negro in New York: An Informal Social History*. New York: New York Public Library, 1967.

Pease, Jane H., and Pease, William A., eds. *The Antislavery Argument*. New York: Bobbs–Merrill, 1965.

————. *The Fugitive Slave Law and Anthony Burns: A Problem in Law Enforcement*. Philadelphia, 1975.

————. *They Who Would Be Free: Blacks' Search for Freedom, 1830-1861*. New York: Atheneum, 1974.

Pessen, Edward. *Jacksonian America: Society, Personality, and Politics*. Homewood, Ill.: Dorsey Press, 1969.

Phillips, U.B. *American Negro Slavery*. 1918. Reprint. Baton Rouge: Louisiana State Univ. Press, 1966.

Potter, David. *The Impending Crisis, 1848-1861*. New York: Harper and Row, 1976.

Quarles, Benjamin. *Black Abolitionists*. New York: Oxford Univ. Press, 1969.

Raboteau, Albert J. "Richard Allen and the African Church Movement." In *Black Leaders of the Nineteenth Century*, pp. 1-18. Edited by Leon F. Litwack and August Meier. Chicago: Univ. of Illinois Press, 1988.

Richards, Leonard. *"Gentleman of Property and Standing": Anti-Abolition Mobs in Jacksonian American*. New York: Oxford Univ. Press, 1970.

Robinson, Donald L. *Slavery in the Structure of American Politics, 1765-1820*. New York: Harcourt Brace Jovanovich, 1971.

Robinson, W. Wright. *A History of Seaford, 1632-1932*. Delmar, Delaware: Red Arrow Press, 1932.

Roland, Charles P. *An American Illiad*. Lexington: Univ. Press of Kentucky, 1991.

Scharf, J. Thomas, and Thompson Westcott. *History of Philadelphia, 1609-1884*. 3 vols. Philadelphia: L.H. Everts, 1884.

Seibert, Wilbur H. *The Underground Railroad from Slavery to Freedom*. 1898. Reprint. New York: Russel and Russel, 1967.

Slaughter, Thomas P. *Bloody Dawn: The Christiana Riot and Racial Violence in the Antelbellum North*. New York: Oxford Univ. Press, 1991.

Smith, Abbot Emerson. *Colonists in Bondage: White Servitude and Convict Labor in America, 1607-1776*. Chapel Hill: Univ. of North Carolina Press, 1947.

Smith, Julia Floyd. *Slavery and Plantation Growth in Antebellum Florida, 1821-60*. Gainesville: University of Florida Press, 1973.

Soderlund, Jean R. *Quakers and Slavery: A Divided Spirit*. Princeton: Princeton Univ. Press, 1985.

Sorin, Gerald. *The New York Abolitionists: A Case Study in Political Radicalism*. Westport, Conn.: Greenwood Press, 1971.

Stampp, Kenneth M. *The Peculiar Institution: Slavery in the Antebellum South*. New York: Vintage, 1956.

Stewart, James Brewer. *Holy Warriors: The Abolitionists and American Slavery*. New York: Hill and Wang, 1976.

Stowe, Harriet Beecher. *Key to Uncle Tom's Cabin*. Boston: John P. Jewett, 1853.

Stroud, George M. *A Sketch of the Laws Relating to Slavery in the Several States of the United States of America.* 2d ed. Philadelphia: Henry Longstreth, 1856.

Taylor, Orville W. *Negro Slavery in Arkansas.* Durham: Duke University Press, 1958.

tenBroek, Jacobus. *Equal Under the Law.* New York: Collier Books, 1965.

Thomas, John L. *The Liberator: William Lloyd Garrison.* Boston: Little, Brown, 1963.

Thornbrough, Emma Lou. *The Negro in Indiana: A Study of a Minority.* Indianapolis: Indiana Historical Bureau, 1957.

Tilden, William P. "Memorial Address Commemorating the 100th Anniversary of the Birth of Thomas Garrett." In *Station Master on the Underground Railroad: The Life and Letters of Thomas Garrett.* By James A. McGowen. Moylan, Pa.: Whimsie Press, 1977.

Townshend, George Alfred. *The Entailed Hat.* 1884. Reprint. Cambridge, Md.: Tidewater Publishing, 1955.

———. *Tales of the Chesapeake.* Cambridge, Md.: Tidewater Publishing, 1968.

Tuckerman, Bayard. *William Jay and the Constitutional Movement for the Abolition of Slavery.* 1893. Reprint. New York: Franklin, 1969.

Turner, Edward Raymond. *The Negro in Pennsylvania: Slavery, Servitude, Freedom, 1739-1861.* 1911. Reprint. New York: Negro Universities Press, 1969.

Tyson, John S. *Life of Elisha Tyson, Philanthropist.* Baltimore: Benjamin Lundy, 1825.

Voegeli, V. Jacque. *Free But Not Equal: The Midwest and the Negro during the Civil War.* Chicago: Univ. of Chicago Press, 1967.

Walters, Ronald G. "The Boundaries of Abolitionism." In *Antislavery Reconsidered: New Perspectives on the Abolitionists,* pp. 3-23. Edited by Lewis Perry and Michael Fellman. Baton Rouge: Louisiana State Univ. Press, 1979.

Warner, Sam Bass, Jr. *The Private City: Philadelphia in Three Periods of Its Growth.* Philadelphia: Univ. of Pennsylvania Press. 1968.

Washburne, E.B. *Sketch of Edward Coles.* Chicago: Jansen, McClurg, 1882.

Weigley, Russell F. *Philadelphia: A 300-Year History.* New York: W.W. Norton, 1982.

Wesley, Charles Harris. *Richard Allen: Apostle of Freedom.* Washington, D.C., Associated Publishers, 1935.

Wiecek, William M. *The Sources of Antislavery Constitutionalism in America, 1760-1848*. Ithaca: Cornell Univ. Press, 1977.

Williams, Eric. "Slavery in the West Indies." In *Slavery: A Comparative Perspective*, pp. 25-37. Edited by Robin W. Winks. New York: New York Univ. Press, 1972.

Wilson, Henry C. *Rise and Fall of the Slave Power*. 3 vols. Boston: Houghton Mifflin, 1872.

Winch, Julie. *Philadelphia's Black Elite: Activism, Accommodation, and the Struggle for Autonomy, 1787-1848*. Philadelphia: Temple Univ. Press, 1988.

Winks, Robin W. *The Blacks in Canada: A History*. New Haven: Yale University Press, 1971.

Wittke, Carl, ed. *The History of the State of Ohio*. Vol. 4, *The Civil War Era, 1850-1873*, by Eugene H. Roseboom. Columbus: Ohio State Archeological and Historical Society, 1944.

Wood, Peter H. *Black Majority: Negroes in Colonial South Carolina from 1670 through the Stono Rebellion*. New York: Alfred A. Knopf, 1974.

Wright, James M. *The Free Negro in Maryland, 1634-1860*. New York: Longmans, Green, 1921.

Zangrando, Robert L. *The NAACP Crusade Against Lynching, 1909-1950*. Philadelphia: Temple Univ. Press, 1980.

Zilversmit, Arthur. *The First Emancipation: The Abolition of Slavery in the North*. Chicago: Univ. of Chicago Press, 1967.

Zimmerman, James Fulton. *Impressment of American Seamen*. New York: Columbia Univ. Press, 1925.

ARTICLES

Bellamy, Donnie D. "The Free Black in Antebellum Missouri, 1820-1860." *Missouri Historical Review* 67 (Jan. 1973): 198-226.

Blue, Frederick J. "Chase and the Governorship: A Stepping Stone to the Presidency." *Ohio History* 90 (Summer 1981): 197-220.

Bolster, W. Jeffrey. "To Feel Like A Man: Black Seamen in the Northern States, 1800-1860." *Journal of American History* 76 (March 1990): 1173-99.

Bridner, Elwood L., Jr. "The Fugitive Slaves of Maryland." *Maryland Historical Magazine* 66 (1971): 33-50.

Calvert, Monte A. "The Abolition Society of Delaware, 1801-1807." *Delaware History* 10 (Oct. 1963): 295-320.

Coldham, Peter Wilson. "The 'Spiriting' of London Children to

Virginia, 1648-1685." *Virginia Magazine of History and Biography* 83 (July 1975): 280-87.

David, C.W.A. "The Fugitive Slave Law of 1793." *Journal of Negro History* 9 (Jan. 1924): 18-24.

Degler, Carl N. "Slavery and the Genesis of American Race Prejudice," *Comparative Studies in Society and History* 2 (Oct. 1959): 49-66.

Dye, Ira. "Early American Merchant Seafarers." *Proceedings of the American Philosophical Society* 120 (1976): 331-34.

Finkelman, Paul. "The Kidnapping of John Davis and the Adoption of the Fugitive Slave Law of 1793." *Journal of Southern History* 56 (Aug. 1990): 397-422.

———. "Prigg v. Pennsylvania and Northern State Courts Antislavery Use of a Pro-slavery Decision." *Civil War History* 25 (March 1979): 5-35.

———. "The Protection of Black Rights in Seward's New York." *Civil War History* 53 (Sept. 1988): 211-34.

Foner, Philip S. "The Battle to End Discrimination Against Negroes on Philadelphia Streetcars." *Pennsylvania History* 40 (July 1973): 261-90.

Fornell, Earl W. "The Abduction of Free Negroes and Slaves in Texas." *Southwestern Historical Quarterly* 60 (Jan. 1957): 369-80.

Freehling, William W. "The Founding Fathers and Slavery." *American Historical Review* 77 (Feb. 1972): 81-93.

Gara, Larry. "William Still and the Underground Railroad." *Pennsylvania History* 28 (Jan. 1961): 33-44.

Goodheart, Lawrence B. "The Chronicles of Kidnapping in New York: Resistance to the Fugitive Slave Law, 1834-1835." *Afro-Americans in New York History and Life* 8 (Jan. 1984): 7-15.

Greene, Lorenzo J. "Prince Hall: Massachusetts Leader in Crisis." *Freedomways* 1 (Fall 1961): 238-58.

Hamer, Philip M. "Great Britain, the United States, and the Negro Seamen Acts, 1822-1848." *Journal of Southern History* 1 (1935): 3-28.

———. "British Consuls and the Negro Seamen Acts, 1850-1860." *Journal of Southern History* 1 (1935): 138-168.

Handlin, Oscar, and Handlin, Mary F. "Origins of the Southern Labor System" *William and Mary Quarterly*, series 3, 7 (April 1950): 199-222.

Hartley, William B. "The Case of the Sobbing Owl." *Cavalier*, Aug. 1954, pp. 31-35.

Hershberg, Theodore. "Free Blacks in Antebellum Philadelphia: A Study of Ex-Slaves, Freeborn, and Socioeconomic Decline." *Journal of Social History* 5 (Winter 1971-72): 183-209.

Landon, Fred. "The Negro Migration to Canada after the Passing of the Fugitive Slave Law." *Journal of Negro History* 5 (Jan. 1920): 22-26.

Leslie, William R. "The Constitutional Significance of Indiana's Statute of 1824 on Fugitives from Labor." *Journal of Southern History* 13 (1947): 338-353.

———. "The Pennsylvania Fugitive Slave Act of 1826." *Journal of Southern History* 18 (Nov. 1952): 429-45.

———. "A Study in the Origins of Interstate Rendition: The Big Beaver Creek Murders." *American Historical Review* 57 (Oct. 1951): 63-76.

Miller, M. Sammy. "Patty Cannon: Murderer and Kidnapper of Free Blacks: A Review of the Evidence." *Maryland Historical Magazine* 72 (Fall 1977): 419-423.

Mulderink, Earl F., III. "'The Whole Town is Ringing With It': Slave Kidnapping Charges Against Nathan Johnson of New Bedford, Massachusetts, 1839." *New England Quarterly* 61 (September 1988): 341-57.

Munroe, John H. "The Negro in Delaware." *South Atlantic Quarterly* 56 (Autumn 1957): 428-44.

Nash, Gary B. "New Light on Richard Allen: The Early Years of Freedom." *William and Mary Quarterly* 46 (1989): 332-40.

Nash, Roderick W. "William Parker and the Christiana Riot." *Journal of Negro History* 46 (Jan. 1961): 24-31.

Porter, Dorothy B. "David M. Ruggles, an Apostle of Human Rights." *Journal of Negro History* 27 (Jan. 1943): 23-50.

Quarles, Benjamin. "Freedom Fettered: Blacks in the Constitutional Era in Maryland, 1776-1810—An Introduction." *Maryland Historical Magazine* 84 (1989): 299-304.

Runcie, John. "Hunting the Nigs in Philadelphia: The Race Riot of August 1834." *Pennsylvania History* 39 (1972): 187-218.

Steel, Edward M., Jr. "Black Monongalians: A Judicial View of Slavery and the Negro in Monongalia County, 1776-1865." *West Virginia History* 34 (July 1973): 331-59.

———. "Bypath to Freedom." *West Virginia History* 31 (Oct. 1969): 33-39.

Tully, Alan. "Patterns of Slaveholding in Colonial Pennsylvania: Chester and Lancaster Counties, 1729-1758." *Journal of Social History* 6 (1973): 284-305.

White, Laura A. "The South in the 1850's as seen by British Consuls." *Journal of Southern History* 1 (1935): 29-48.

Williams, Irene E. "The Operation of the Fugitive Slave Law in Western Pennsylvania from 1850 to 1860." *Western Pennsylvania Historical Magazine* 4 (1921): 150-60.

Wilson, Benjamin C. "Kentucky Kidnappers, Fugitives, and Abolitionists in Antebellum Cass County, Michigan." *Michigan History* 60 (Winter 1976): 339-58.

Winch, Julie. "Philadelphia and the Other Underground Railroad." *Pennsylvania Magazine of History and Biography* 111 (Jan. 1987): 3-25.

Dissertation

Essah, Patience. "Slavery and Freedom in the First State: The History of the Black in Delaware from the Colonial Period to 1865." Ph.D. diss., University of California, Los Angeles, 1985.

Index

"Abe" (kidnapped slave), 122 n 13
abolitionism: effect of racism on, 99-102; gradualism channeled into colonization movement, 99; immediatism replaced gradualism, 97-99
abolitionists. *See* individual names
abolition organizations. *See also* American Convention of Abolition Societies
—activities of: blacks initially excluded, 104; decline after 1820s, 96-102; difficulties faced by, 19-20, 94-95; direct involvement in individual cases, 91-94; lobby for federal antikidnapping law, 89; lobby for state laws, 87-88; names of reflect concern about kidnapping, 83; provide financial assistance for victims, 84, 93-94; publish manumission records, 86-87; Quakers' role in, 83, 85-86, 89; request assistance of federal government, 89-90, 95
—individual societies: Arlington (Va.), 86, 91; Alexandria (Va.), 86, 91; Chestertown (Md.), 91; Choptank (Md.), 84, 86, 90; Connecticut, 85, 91; Delaware, 17, 83, 84, 86, 87-88, 91-92, 94, 95, 97; Kentucky, 85, 91; Maryland, 19, 83, 86, 87, 90; New Jersey, 84, 90; New York Manumission Society, 84, 90, 97;

North Carolina Manumission Society, 84; Pennsylvania, 19, 20, 21, 22, 26-27, 51, 52, 83-96, 97, 104; Philanthropic Society of Easton (Md.), 84; Richmond (Va.), 94; Rhode Island, 91; Virginia, 86, 91, 95; Washington (D.C.), 91, Wilmington (Del.), 90; Winchester (Va.), 91
African Observer, 17, 118
Albany (N.Y.) Evening Journal, 56
Alberti, George (kidnapper), 50-53
Allen, Richard (victim), 106, 107
Allen, William (abolitionist), 65
American Colonization Society, 99
American Convention of Abolition Societies, 18, 84, 85, 89, 94-95, 97
American Negro Slavery, 6
Amos, Charles (victim), 15
anti-immigration laws, 40; passed by many states and territories, 57; prohibited blacks from entering a state, 30, 57; protests against, 57-58
antikidnapping laws, 51; attempts to strengthen in Del., 68-69, 87-88; call for passage of federal, 69-71, 89; call for passage of in Md., 68, 87; call for passage of in Pa., 87; lack of effectiveness, 67; passage of federal, 71;